Dalits and Economic Reforms

Dalits and Economic Reforms

Edited by
ARUN KUMAR

RAWAT PUBLICATIONS
Jaipur • New Delhi • Bangalore • Mumbai • Hyderabad • Guwahati

ISBN 81-316-0307-5

Published by
Prem Rawat for **Rawat Publications**
Satyam Apts, Sector 3, Jawahar Nagar, Jaipur 302 004 (India)
Phone: 0141 265 1748 / 7006 Fax: 0141 265 1748
E-mail: info@rawatbooks.com
Website: www.rawatbooks.com

New Delhi Office
4858/24, Ansari Road, Daryaganj, New Delhi 110 002
Phone: 011 2326 3290

Also at Bangalore, Mumbai, Hyderabad and Guwahati

Typeset by Rawat Computers, Jaipur
Printed at Nice Printing Press, New Delhi

Dedicated

to

the Goddess

MAA BALA TRIPUR SUNDARI

(Jagdamba Nagar, Barhiya)

Bihar

Contents

Foreword

India has a glorious past. The cultural heritage of India has been very rich. But a large section of its civilized and cultured society has been, for age-long neglected, depraved and exploited. The depraved class is still living under such a social status where socio-economic, political, educational and psychological upliftment has no scope. This adverse condition has been a great obstacle in bringing out the prosperity for all in Indian society. Under the yoke of the British rule, this condition became more adverse and Indian thinkers were forced to think over the condition of this neglected and depraved class. As a consequence, after the independence, members of our Constituent Assembly adopted many provisions in Indian Constitution to protect the interest of the depraved class. They were of the view that a guaranteed protection will help in bringing out the overall development of the country. It would add to the national integrity and security. That was the reason why the concept of a welfare state was adopted in which a democratic society could strive for equality and social justice.

One of the best concepts of modern world is social justice. Its aim and objective is to imagine such a society in which opportunity and duties of a citizen are based on equality and the interest of each citizen is protected through a proper distribution of the resources. The main factor of social justice is liberty and equality, that is, an absence of obstacles and discrimination. But, in this system, elements of liberty and equality tends to become partial instead of being impartial. If the freedom of a prosperous is the cause of the poverty of the hapless poor, the delimitation of the freedom of the prosperous is not the rejection of the principle of freedom, it is an act of compliance. In the same way, if a society is divided on the basis of birth, origin, caste and class, there is no practical value of the principle of equality and social justice. In this situation, to give protection to hapless poor and depraved is not the refusal of the principle of equality and social justice, it is an act of compliance.

Social justice has two aspects—growth and distribution. In a liberal and capitalist society, the ability of an individual is considered the basis of proper distribution, and the individual strives to become more able in order to gain more and more. Socialists consider that the basis of distribution must be equality not the ability. The distribution must meet the need of every individual. Neo-liberalist and welfare state concepts emphasize to bring a harmony in growth and distribution for social justice. Accordingly, the facilities should be given to all in the society to meet their fundamental requirement.

Post-independent India accepted the concept of a welfare state with socialistic and mixed economic system. With a view of upbringing the depraved classes and establishing equality in society, the government launched and implemented many policies. Efforts were continued for decades but the expected results were not achieved and with the fall of USSR, the nation which followed the Russian model of economic system, fell into a financial crunch in the eighties. Social harmony was still in its childhood. To cope with this situation, India adopted the new economic policy based on western model suggested by IMF and the World Bank. The New Economic Policy alongwith the New Industrial Policy was adopted on 24th July, 1991. After independence, throwing away the controlled and regulated economic system, the open market economy is being adopted. Today, it is believed that the main three factors of New Economic Policy—Liberalization, Privatization and Globalization—will resolve all the problems.

The short-term goal of the New Economic Policy is to take away the nation from the financial instability and crunch. For this, the nation has to take some measures—to enhance the gross income through making a balance between demand and supply, to lessen the expenditure of the establishment, to control black money and to adopt an effective taxation system. The mid-term goal of this policy is to make the economy of the country self-reliant. The nation has to make the industries competitive. An effective measure has to be taken for bringing out the reforms in issuing license for industries. Through an effective reform in regulations and infrastructure and opening up the market for the world trade, the objectives may be achieved. The long-term goals can be made possible through a proper distribution of the profit based on social justice.

This is a well-known fact that the role of economy is very significant in socio-cultural construct of any society. Here, it is worth considering whether the New Economic Policy is in agreement with the declared socio-economic objectives and constitutional ideals or not. The New Economic Policy gives an emphasis on development. Does it provide development for all in real sense? Does this policy provide a system where a proper distribution of the profit may be possible in future? In what ways this policy will have an impact on depraved class? Does this policy encourage a system where the objectives of the concept of social justice can be achieved? In this perspective, a national seminar sponsored by University Grant Commission on the topic *The New Economic Policy: Its Impact on Dalits* was held and it became a platform for and against this policy. A significant debate and discourse was delivered on different issues like reservation in New Economic Policy, small-scale and domestic industries, employment, agriculture, education and health, civilization and culture, morality and psychological analysis of Dalits. All these issues were discussed with a view to their impact on Dalits and the New Economic Policy.

Reservation policy gives a protection to depraved classes in order to give them opportunities to progress. On the other hand, liberalization and privatization in the New Economic Policy refutes the policy to protect the interest of depraved classes. Though, economic reforms have generated the possibilities of a development in small-scale industries, it has also created a violent competition and endangered the traditional way of employment and opportunities for Dalits. Modern technology and communication system have created hopes and aspirations which has been resulted in emergence of huge national and multinational companies. These companies have made such a competitive atmosphere where Dalits have no prospects at all, and here arises the question of the existence of Dalits. The opportunities of employment in public sector has become lessened, whereas the private sector is providing more and more jobs, but due to certain bias and discrimination which they are facing for centuries, Dalits are devoid of getting employment in private sector. This problem has become more worsened due to the privatization in education and medical services. Today, students belonging to Dalit class can hardly get admission to higher education like medical science, engineering, management and professional courses. It has added to the intensity of the crisis.

Due to this policy, India will face crucial problems like widening social and economical inequality, which ultimately will lead India into the realm of social clashes and upheavals. Dalit classes are pushed in such a condition where they are facing a threat to their traditional way of earning their livelihood due to cut-throat competition of monstrous companies and industries. The state also is withdrawing from where it is to safeguard the traditional and domestic industries. If protection is not provided by the state, the condition of Dalit class will never be improved.

However, a balanced synchronization of traditional and domestic system and New Economic Policy can bridge the gap and lead India to transform her into a developed nation where social inequality will have no place. This is, indeed, the need of the hour. I hope this book will benefit the academics, social reformers and policy makers. The book may play a vital role in order to bring social justice in India.

S.K. Thorat
Chairman
University Grants Commission
New Delhi

Preface

Fundamental structure of Indian society—divided in castes and sub-castes hailed from birth—is based on inequality. In this division, pad-trodden depraved Dalits are at the lowest. Their past is unhappy and their identity also is unfortunate. Baba Saheb Ambedkar says, "Hindu society is like that multistoreyed tower which has no gate or stair for entry; he who borns in a storey, has to die in the same storey". Though many a social reformers have taken pain to bring a reform in order to improve the condition of Dalits, they are still in a miserable condition.

After independence, the Constitution of India established the principle of liberty and equality by eradicating the customary discrimination between the privileged and depraved in every sphere of social life. Apart from this, many provisions were brought in the Constitution in order to bring social justice, upliftment and security for Dalits. Related to this, some main provisions as Article 14, 15, 16, 19, 23, 29, 164, 275, 330, 332, 334, 338, 339, 342, 366, fifth and sixth schedule are provided in the Constitution. Keeping these provisions in view, many a schemes and plannings were launched. As a result social, political, economic and educational condition of Dalits was improved. They were led towards development. When their development was in its infancy, Indian economy faced a crunch in 1980s. To cope with this problem New Industrial Policy was implemented on 24th July, 1991 and New Economic Policy was, thus, introduced. The previous economic policy was criticized and it was said that the economic policy was highly controlled. It was also said that the country witnessed a greater loss than the profit.

The aim and objective of New Economic Policy is to bring reform in public treasury and to open Indian economy for international competition by restructuring public sector units. Instead of extremely controlled and regulated economic policy like licensing, quota and permit raj, a market-based economic policy has to be implemented which may enable to conduct economic activities based on demand and supply, and to enable the industries to become competent internationally and to open Indian economy for world trade. This will enhance competency, productivity and above all, expertise and quality.

The implementation of the New Economic Policy has witnessed more than a decade and it is being considered that each and every problem has its solution in the three factors of the policy—Liberalization, Privatization and Globalization. Keeping this perspective in minds, an idea of a National Seminar on the topic, "New Economic Policy and Its Impact on Dalits" sponsored by UGC, CRO Bhopal, was conceived and many a papers were presented in this regard. The publication of presented standard papers in a book form, has an intention to bring out the real perspective of Indian sensibility to the mind of our policy makers, which, ultimately will help and pave a way to expedite the schemes for the upliftment of Dalits.

In the first preference, I extend my gratitude to University Grant Commission that sponsored to do this solemn piece of work.

Sharad Chandra Behar, IAS, ex-Chief Secretary, MP Government; former Vice Chancellor, Pt. Makhan Lal Chaturvedi Patrakarita University, Bhopal (MP); former Vice Chancellor, Guru Ghasidas University, Bilaspur (C.G.) gave me his expert suggestions and valuable cooperation at every level. I feel, it is my duty to be thankful to him.

The very first citizen of Katni city, Sandeep Jaiswal gave me his opinion and valuable cooperation in order to organize the seminar. I am thankful to him.

Anupam Rajan, IAS, the then Collector of Katni gave me his valuable suggestions and provided me all cooperation at every level which led my programme to success. I am thankful to him.

I am also grateful to famous social scientist, Ram Gopal Singh who gave his precious advise to achieve this goal.

I am grateful to S.N. Choudhary, Rajiv Gandhi Professor, Rajiv Gandhi Chair in Contemporary Studies. Barkatullah University, Bhopal, too for his kind cooperation.

Sohan Pal Sumanakshar, President, Bhartiya Dalit Sahitya Academy, Delhi, Hari Mohan Dhavan and Poonam Chand Bairwa, President and Secretary, Madhya Pradesh Dalit Sahitya Academy, Ujjain, extended their support and their views on the topic, which became a source of inspiration to me. I am thankful to all of them.

I solemnly extend my gratitude to A.P.S. Chauhan, Head, Political Science Department, Jeewaji University, Gwalior, Shyam Kashyap, Head, Department of Journalism, Delhi University, Delhi, Shrinath Sharma, Department of Sociology, Dr Hari Singh Gaur University, Sagar, Shailesh Chaubey, Head, Department of Economics, Rani Durgawati University, Jabalpur, R.D. Maurya and D.K. Verma, Dr Baba Saheb Ambedkar Social Science Research Institute, Mhow (Indore) for their suggestions.

Senior journalist and famous social worker, Nand Lal Singh, actively supported and extended his helping hand towards me to bring this programme to a success.

Saroj Modi, ex-Principal and Ila Ghosh, Principal, Government Tilak P.G. College, Katni gave me all kind of support to bring this work in a book form. I am thankful to them.

I am especially thankful to my colleagues for their cooperation without which this work could never be possible. I am grateful to Ashok Shrivastava, G.M. Mustafa and Kumar Jainendra Sinha for their exhaustive cooperation in publication of this book.

I am grateful to all the scholars who presented their original and valuable articles for this book.

I personally feel my gratitude towards my parents, aunty and uncle, whose love and affection has been always a source of inspiration to me. I especially remember my elder brother, Sunil Kumar, Lecturer in Political Science, SBR College, Bardh, Bihar, who bestowed his love and affection on me, has recently passed away. His journey to heavenly abode has left such an impression on me that cannot be, in any manner, subdued. I am also very much thankful to my wife Veena Singh, Assistant Professor of Chemistry, Government Girls College, Katni (MP) who actively cooperated with me in all spheres of life.

Last but not the least, I extend my cordial gratefulness to Pranit Rawat, Rawat Publications who showed a lot of interest in the subject and undertook a task to publish the book on such a contemporary issue.

Arun Kumar

Contributors

S.N. Choudhary, Rajiv Gandhi Chair, Barkatullah University, Bhopal.

D.K. Verma, Head, Division of SC, ST and OBC Development, Ambedkar National Institute of Social Science, Mhow (MP).

Niraj Kumar Jha, Assistant Professor of Political Science, MLB College, Gwalior (MP).

Akhilesh K. Sharma, Assistant Professor of Political Science, Government P.G. Autonomous College, Satna (MP).

Lokesh K. Prasad, Assistant Professor, Department of Political Science, Government M.K.B. Arts and Commerce Autonomous College for Women, Jabalpur (MP).

Bijoy Kumar, Sr. Lecturer, Postgraduate Department of Political Science, S.K.M. University, Dumka (Jharkhand).

Ranjana Mishra, Head, Department of Political Science, Hitkarini Mahila Mahavidyalaya, Jabalpur.

Sunil K. Shrivastava, Assistant Professor of Political Science, Government College, Paatan, Jabalpur.

Mahavir Prasad Modi, Assistant Professor of Political Science, Government Girls College, Morena (MP).

Bidya Shankar Bibhuti, Assistant Professor of Political Science, B.S.N. Government P.G. College, Shajapur (MP).

Sanjeev K. Sinha, Sr. Lecturer, P.G. Department of Political Science, S.K.M. University, Dumka.

Ratnesh Kishore Verma, Assistant Professor of Poltical Science, Government Tilak P.G. College, Katni (MP).

G.M. Mustafa, Assistant Professor of English, Government Tilak P.G. College, Katni.

Jainendra Yadav, Sr. Lecturer, P.G. Department of Political Science, S.K.M. University, Dumka (Jharkhand).

Chitra Prabhat, Assistant Professor of Political Science, Government Tilak P.G. College, Katni.

Gopal K. Singh, Head, Department of Political Science, S.P. College, Dumka.

K.J. Sinha, Assistant Professor of Economics, Government Tilak P.G. College, Katni.

Sunil Bajpayee, Assistant Professor of Commerce, Government Tilak P.G. College, Katni.

Jay Shankar Sharma, Lecturer, Department of Commerce, Evening College, Delhi University, New Delhi.

1

In between Local Culture and Globalization

S.N. CHOUDHARY

The paper intends to examine the nature and role of local culture in the mitigation of the problems of common people, especially the excluded in India in the historical perspective. It also explores how due to globalization process, the Indian economy became powerful but at the same time, it contributed to the weakening of the culture-centric coping mechanisms used by the masses to overcome crisis. Finally, the paper suggest some mechanisms of rural development which, without hurting the process of globalization, may be beneficial for the common man.

I

Local culture, found especially in the rural and tribal India, implies historically not only ways of life but also crisis management mechanism. And it has remained more and more effective and powerful among the communities which are at the lower level of the development ladder in the modern economic sense of the term. It has helped them to manage crisis in different walks of life. In spite of the fact, that Indian culture is highly heterogeneous and area specific and today the process of acculturation is very fast, but in spite of that, culture is inevitable in the life of common man. People living in the same village worship different gods and goddesses, have different food habits, political affiliations, carry different social identities and so on. This shows richness of Indian culture.

Conceptually, local culture is local in terms of its origin as well as its functioning. Hence, it is space specific and social groups specific. It has long history. It is constructed and deconstructed by the users on the basis of their felt and perceived experience. Since, people even at the so-called local level are also heterogeneous therefore, they have some distinct cultural traits, but the core values and core foundation of the culture working at the local level is common. For example, at the time of death, accident, theft, fire, etc., people at the local level, across their socio-economic variations, cooperate each other. This is the feature of local culture in the rural and tribal areas of this country. It is the moral responsibility of each of the household not to allow even the beggar to go unattended. Relatives of one family equally commend respect in the neighbourhood. Nobody is allowed to stave in an average village in India. How this net of social relationship is affected by the globalization process? This is one among several questions of social importance, which need to be examined to determine nature of relationship between globalization and the marginalized.

Impact of Globalization on Culture

It is needless to mention here that the dream of human rights embodied in the French revolution has shaped history throughout the world. The socialist dream coming out of the former USSR became a powerful ideology in many countries. Some of the great religions of the world such as Buddhism have spread by force of ideas and not because of the gun power. Gandhi drew inspiration from Christianity and Western democracy. English education helped freedom fighters to create public opinion against British imperialism in many countries. Martin Luther King Jr. drew inspiration from Gandhi and Nehru and Luther also inspired both leaders. These are few examples of diffusion of noble ideas and values.

But, today, the free flow of information does not contain such noble ideas and values directed to the cause of humanity. Currently, under the globalization regime, information is perceived as a commodity which is subject to purchase and sale. It has negatively affected social and cultural heritage of many countries, including

India. Even one developed nation is attacked by another without hesitation. This is an example of cultural invasion through powerful ideas. The nations which have failed to generate powerful ideas and sold them successfully, they are bound to suffer and to be dependent. This is clear from the following examples:

1. The presence of American films and TV shows are obvious throughout the world. Even the outdated American films and serials are earning huge money throughout the world. It is worthwhile to mention that in South Africa and Sahara there is no indigenous publication industry. This work is only done by the British and French publishers. Whatever the children read in African countries mostly it is edited in London and Paris with no test of local examples. TV news production is very expensive. If the broadcasting is round the clock it becomes more costly. There is total monopoly of CNN, BBC, STAR PLUS, etc., on the TV screen. These channels hardly concentrate on status of women in Pakistan, child labour in India and East Bengal, poverty in Nepal, bride burning in India and so on. Most often these and other channels propagate consumer culture. For example, today throughout the West Africa one can see advertisement for skin-lightening creams. Further, we are failed to see even a single dark-skinned model on Indian screens, magazines and other advertisements. Nexus between consumer ethic and television may be realized from the fact that in USA, the multinational corporations spent on advertisement alone is over half of what all the nations of the world combined, spend on education.
2. Globalization is indirectly influencing our way of life by influencing the film industry. It is needless to mention that out of 4,000 feature films, shown annually on Brazilian TV, 90 per cent are made in either USA or Europe. Even in the developed countries like Canada about more than 97 per cent films shown in the theatres are foreign made, mostly in the America. According to one observation, through these films, America is successful in spreading a specific type of culture which suits to its capitalistic ideology and help to retain its hegemony, but it do not share a culture of debate, dissent and discussion which it encourages in the classroom in its own country.

Protest and Outcome

Attempts have been made to stop culture invasion by both the developed and the developing countries but significant improvement is yet to take place. For example, France adopted two techniques to stop culture invasion. More than any country in the world it subsidized the arts, including film industry. Further, it adopted the European guideline that at least half of what is shown on European TV must be produced in Europe. But partly because of spread of English language in France and CNN, the French effort did not succeed.

In India, an indirect effort was made to encounter cultural invasion by producing two most popular TV serials, *Ramayana* and *Mahabharata*. But, its impact did not create ground in favour of the indigenous culture. These serials could not stop cultural invasion. Many of the Hindi films could not get itself free from foreign colour. For instance, the Hindi movie *Dil to Pagal Hai* was made without any multinational hand. But, minute examination of its content and story clearly reveal that the plot was borrowed from an American film, there is no Indian street scene, the dress of hero-heroine is totally western. Hero-heroine consume mineral water, Japanese food and Pepsi drink. In fact, this is an Indian film without India in it. Whether, globalization has succeeded at the economic front or not is a controversial issue because it has been failed to generate employment opportunities, put check on the devaluation of the Indian economy, promote export and reduce import, contributed to suicide among farmers, contributed to price rise and rural violence and so on, but it is beyond doubt that it has adversely affected local culture and way of life of common people. Here, it would be proper to say that the poor and the marginalized are more and more dependent on local culture for their crisis management and if there is erosion of their cultural heritage they are bound to be straw man because they cannot avail benefits of new facilities for want of resources. As an ideology, globalization pleads for infrastructure development as the pre-condition for other development and do not address the problems of basic health, basic education, food and livelihood security, problem of corruption and price rise, untouchability and child labour, effective functioning of PDS, etc., therefore, many scholars perceive it anti-poor. According to one observation, one US dollar was equivalent to Rs 4.76 in 1947, but it became equivalent to Rs 42 during 1998. Also, 1988–89 and 90–91, 12 lakh people got employment but during 1991–92–93 only 2 lakh people got jobs. Closure of different undertakings/concerns by the government, reduction in subsidies, introduction of voluntary retirement scheme, all these show gross failure of the New Economic Policy at the economic front. Media is today completely playing in the hands of those who are popularizing consumer culture. A new test and food habit is emerging which is not at all local. It is governed by the international dictation. The tradition of folk art, culture, storytelling and the role of local talents in its popularization is giving way to jug and mug culture. According to one observation, consumer goods are now very easily available on credit with zero interest rate. The practice of post-dated cheque is becoming culture and those who enter into this trap, most often it is difficult for them to break the trap. But how many people can afford this lifestyle? How many of us can follow Cola-Cola culture? Those who are unable to imitate it, they are frustrated. However, it is apprehended that in the urban areas even the slum and pavement dwellers are influenced, by the market forces. If their purse do not permit to follow the dictation of the market forces, a section of them is even ready to adopt it by following illegal practices. Even a section of urban middle-class youth is running behind this culture without having resource facility. Tribal youth having exposure to outside world are developing disrespect in favour of their culture and way of life. In short, today almost the entire urban India is forced to follow consumer culture without understanding its short and long-term negative consequences. This is likely to increase the number of crime. Unfortunately, there is no protest against imposition of such alien culture on the Indian society. There is *Swadesi Jagran Manch* intervention but it is highly temporal, localized, selective, weak and directionless. It is a middle class phenomenon. Poor are away from the *Manch.*

Challenges

Under the given situation, when the collective spirit of Indian culture is being replaced by individualism and people at large are either knowingly or unknowingly showing disinclination towards their tradition and culture in favour of new way of life which is significantly alien for many, the state has to come forward in an assertive manner. The new economic policy or what may be called 'globalization' as a process has strengthen Indian economy and as per RBI report saving of foreign currency in the country which was equivalent to US$ 16,52,750 lakh on 5th October, 2006 has increased to US$ 24,35,240 lakh in 2007, but this growth is broadly without development. It has to be inclusive. If it is not inclusive, it will widen the gap between social groups and regions which is neither healthy for the globalization forces nor for the common citizens of this country who are rapidly loosing their culture as a coping mechanism.

Currently, critics of globalization feel that it will become a threat to political sovereignty, economic and technological independence, social structure and culture and so on. The coalition among the world will widen the gap between the rich and the poor in every nation where globalization spreads. To them, market forces will lead to higher growth rate and higher surplus reserve but the state will not invest more and more on social sectors to protect the interests of the poor.

To them, the reform process which started in 1991 resulted in the contraction of public sector and ascending of the private sector, which in turn has began to dismantle the limited protection being granted to the marginalized in the field of employment. Globalization will drastically narrow down poor's access to basic means of sustenance and development such as education, health, employment, food security and so on. With globalization, there will be either no or limited statutory mechanism to redress grievances of poor and the marginalized, especially when they are the victims of exploitation by the concerns from outside the country.

Ray of Hope

How to regulate the forces of globalization in the interest of common people? Looking to the political behaviour of all the political parties in favour of the ongoing process of globalization, the ray of hope is not possible from them.

The NGO movement is too weak to deal with it. Their movement against ecological crisis caused due to mega-development projects is local and it do not carry mass support in a sustainable manner. Most of the NGOs are now engaged in so-called capacity building of the masses. Hardly concerted pressure is put on the state in favour of inclusive development. Hence, solution is only expected from the victims of globalization. There should be awareness generation programme among the marginalized groups about the negative consequences of globalization, particularly on the marginalized groups, on constant basis. Collective level protest by the current and the expected victims is one of the mechanisms to deal with the problem. The existing and the upcoming people's and democratic organizations at the micro-level may effectively work as an intervention. If the locals are united their agitation may slightly stop the negative rays of globalization.

But, this is an extreme proposition. The victims or their spokesperson may also be divided on multiple bases. Illiteracy, casteism, corruption, communal feeling, limited awareness, poverty, etc., may hinder unity and protest by the victims.

Looking to this historical limitation, a middle path may also be experimented. Why not to capacitate people at large with the pre-conditions/requirements of globalization? Let us take the case of tribes. Tribes have their cultural heritage. Such heritage may be exhibited at different places with the facilitating support of the government. Say, for instance, if they organize exhibitions of their artefacts at different places, it may attract market resulting thereby improvement in their economy. In the same way, they may be trained to use/handle new equipment like the use and repair of computer, internet, mobile phone, etc., and in this way they may become a part of globalization. As a cultural heritage, they have indigenous knowledge. Why not to integrate this knowledge with the new knowledge system in their interest? Why not they are engaged with the value-added manufacturing process? Why not the relevant and effective elements of their culture are marketed at different levels. Today, this intervention is materially possible in a better way because state is now more powerful in comparison to the past in the economic sense.

Since, due to globalization, rate of economic growth of the country reached to 9.4 per cent during 2006–07 and bulk is coming from the service sector, the contribution of agriculture which directly feed about 65 per cent population of the country, have come down to about 1.8 per cent today. It has just grew at the rate of 2.7 per cent in the previous fiscal. At the micro level, this development has degenerated agriculture both as an occupation and as a source of livelihood. Hence, globalization has widened gap between India and *Bharat,* between villages and cities, between rich and the poor. Some economists apprehend that since, agriculture contributes just 18.5 per cent of India's GDP, its slow growth will not act as a drag on the entire economy. They are mistaken. Rural India still accounts for 60 per cent of the country's population and can vote governments out of power if it perceives that growth is not helping people at large. If this happens, it may upset policy momentum and business settlement. If people's requirements are properly addressed, it will besides integrating them with the market forces will help to stabilize industrial demand over time, creating the right climate for investment. For this purpose, following suggestions may be implemented with catholic spirit.

Steps to be Taken

1. In India one-third of total food produce is wasted each year for want of proper storage and marketing facilities. The total cost of this wastage is about Rs 58,000 crore. Of the produce that survives, very little is processed, compared to the situation in Malaysia, the Philippines, Brazil and Thailand. It is here that the entry of the organized retail can make a huge difference. There is an urgent need of creation of large, efficient cold storages which in turn, could transform the character of the food processing industry by enabling it to deal in large volumes. At present, food processing is dominated by the small-scale sector, which is not equipped to deal either in volumes or variety of produce. In the absence of storage systems, these units do not operate round the year yet, it is remarkable that this sector employs about 1.5 million people. It is often overlooked that the Indian agriculture sector is almost totally private. However, it belongs to the realm of the unorganized sector and as such lacks both capital and organizational skills to maximize returns. What is needed is to create a mutually beneficial synthesis between organized private capital as represented by, say, ITC or Wal-Mart and the amorphous agrarian sector. The government should play its legitimate role as an honest broker to help both parties work out an advantageous deal for all concerned. This

could be done by ensuring that there are no job losses, that food prices are both remunerative and stable, and the small agriculturist is saved from suicidal debt.

2. Due to growing degree and amount of acculturation in villages, both urbanism and modernism as a way of life are spreading at a faster rate. Today, villagers need more than connectivity. They need law, order and justice. They need basic education and health. The government is throwing money at the problem instead of reforming these sectors to ensure that teachers and health staff are accountable to the people they serve. Rural areas will be empowered provided Panchayats are extended the right to hire, fire and discipline absentee teachers and health staff but nobody dares do that. The government plans to double spending without structural reform, and this will largely be a waste of money that creates neither skills nor empowerment. There is need to bring poor out of the poverty trap and not to make them dependent through so-called subsidies which is captured by the local rich in the name of poverty eradication. Unfortunately, Rural Employment Schemes have miserably failed to deal with poverty. It is apprehended that the same may happen to the much publicized Rural Employment Guarantee Scheme.

   How to deal with the problem of poverty? Can we move from labour-intensive development scheme to capital-intensive project? Can we plead for all season *pucca* road everywhere instead of labour-intensive temporary roads? *Bharat Nirman* Project aims to provide road, electricity, telecom and drinking water to every village with a population over 1,000 and create one crore additional hectares of irrigation. This project needs to be strengthened.

3. There is need to propagate second Green Revolution with the support from both the government and globalization forces. If the corporate world is entrusted with this responsibility, it is assumed that a second Green Revolution, focussing on fruits and vegetables, can double agricultural growth to 4 per cent per year. For this purpose, contract farming, if not the corporate farming, may be popularized. The biggest rural initiative comes from ITC, whose E-Choupals will cover 1,00,000 villages by 2010, accounting for two-thirds of rural GDP. E-Choupals are electronic buying and selling places, which also provide

information to farmers on prices, weather and scientific farming practices. This intervention will remove the role of middlemen and *Mandi* and will directly benefit the farmers. Already there are number of concerns such as Field Fresh of Sunil Mittal which have already taken 1,000 acre under horticulture in Punjab. Pepsi and McDonalds have started contract farming of citrus fruits and lettuce respectively, Godrej is into contract cultivation of maize to make cattle feed, Global Green, a Thapar Company uses contract cultivation for gherkins and other products for export and has a turnover of over Rs 100 crore. There are many more such examples. However, such steps must be encouraged keeping in view local social and ecological concerns so that the process may be inclusive and sustainable for all.

4. Even today, in spite of an era of privatization, most of the school going children living in the villages having agriculture, trade, wage work in an unorganized sector outside the village as the main source of livelihood of their father, are enrolled in poorly managed village level government schools. Historical experience reveal that with the governmentalization of schools coupled with so-called deeliteization there is deresponsibilization on the part of schools. Teachers are permanent government employees. Most of them are posted in their home districts. They go to school after finishing their farm/home work. It is observed that instead of being accountable to the community they are accountable to the school inspectors posted at the block level. Panchayat has failed to put pressure on the teachers because the local level elites, in case they live in the villages, do not send their children in these schools. The net result is poor teaching in terms of quality. The products of these schools are not in a position to avail and sustain quality education. In one of our recent studies on *Sarva Siksha Abhiyan* and its functioning in Madhya Pradesh, we found that more than 50 per cent students of class 4th and 5th who were interviewed do not know the name of capital of India, capital of Madhya Pradesh, name of prime minister, name of chief minister of Madhya Pradesh, date of independence day and the name of Iron Man of India. Similarly, they do not know simple English, simple mathematics and simple science. More than 92 per cent students also do not know the total number of

districts in Madhya Pradesh and also they do not know the name of state where famous poet Makhan Lal Chaturvedhi was born. How products of these schools with having low level of knowledge can pursue quality improvement of their skill and capabilities and subsequently reap benefits of development? This challenge needs urgent attention. For this purpose, following efforts may be made:

At the very outset, through training and orientation, parents may be made aware about the long-term importance of education in the life of their children and the entire family. They have to be convinced that tomorrow the nature of society will be what may be called 'knowledge based'. We strongly believe that without conscentization of parents other supportive interventions like Mid-Day Meal (MDM), free bicycle, dress and teaching and learning materials to the students will have only limited impact. The responsibility of awareness generation may be entrusted to local level NGOs. Secondly, each year all the teachers should be asked to attend fifteen-days training and orientation programme during summer vacation. Training modules must be area and target group specific. Annual increment of teachers should be based on attendance of students and teachers as well as their performance in the annual examination. Also, a new experiment may be attempted. Ten per cent students from each of the schools belonging to one Gram Panchayat or neighbouring villages may be selected. One coaching centre with having villages as the catchment area may be identified. Three or four local level educated and unemployed youth may be identified. They should be properly trained every now and then at the district level. Today except summer, in each season schools begin at 10:30 am. The 10 per cent selected students may be intensively taught and trained between 7:30 am to 9:30 am at the village level by the trained youths mentioned above. The teaching work may be organized at the private residence/Panchayat Bhavan, etc. Attempt shall be made to teach the students the lesson/chapters in advance, which are to be taught at school during the same day. It is presumed, that if students are already familiar with the content they will be relatively more attentive in the classroom resulting thereby qualitative improvement in teaching and learning. Each year monitoring and evaluation of this experiment may be made to seek feedback for needful modification. If the result is positive the entire students of the experimental schools may be covered in a phased manner as well as this experiment may be replicated elsewhere. Also, there are hundreds of private schools/coaching centres, etc., working in the villages. Large number of retired school teachers are residing in the villages. It is not harmful to seek support of this resource even on contract basis. They may be contracted to ensure enrolment of all children, discourage drop out, strengthen quality education, etc., within a specific time frame. There are hundreds of temples with *Pujari* facility in the villages. These *Pujaris* are culturally accepted and command due respect in the community. There is no harm if these *Pujaris* are occasionally trained to teach children and also to increase level of knowledge of villagers regarding importance of literacy and education in the life of their children.

5. So far as health question is concerned, it needs an urgent intervention. Most of the diseases are initially common. These are either water-based, air-based or both. Today, to get cure of such diseases, people at large depend on *Jhola Chap* doctors in the villages. They are found historically in large number in villages. They are not formally trained. They have learnt something through trial and error and experience. Critically speaking, they are not skilled enough to treat properly but since long they are extending service. People have faith in them and therefore their presence is culturally and socially accepted. There is face-to-face relationship between so-called doctors and the patients. Both are usually local. Many times they treat on credit. Even medicine is provided on credit. Such doctors are available every time. People totally depend on them. Looking to the grass-roots level situation a recommendation may be made. Why not to capacitate these doctors? All such doctors should be registered. They should be provided at least four times training in each year. Training consisting of 100 doctors should be imparted at the district level free of cost. Each training period should be of not less than one week. They should be taught basics of health and diseases by the subject experts. They should also be advised that in case of failure, where they should refer the patient. Since,

they are already culturally accepted in the locality, their advise will be followed by the villagers without hesitation. This experiment is also required because today there is shortage of trained MBBS doctors in the villages. Even if they are posted, they perceive posting as a punishment and accordingly, they try their best to get transferred resulting thereby continued dependence of villagers on *Jhola Chap* doctor. Primary Health Centres (PHC) were started with great hope but it remained invisible and ineffective at the functional level. Hence, it is suggested that instead of thinking to abolish traditional institution or to keep away from it, it would be better to capacitate these doctors and integrate them with the new health saving practices looking to the purchasing power of cross-section of villagers. After functioning of this experiment for two years, evaluation should be made for feedback and subsequently the success story may be replicated elsewhere.

There are other traditional health saving institutions and practices which needs promotion with monetization. Medicinal importance of herbs, leafs, plants, trees should be popularized. Importance of environmental cleanliness should be popularized. Yoga needs to be popularized. Also, in each of the schools playground/game facility should be made available. Cricket is very popular today. But other traditional games should also be promoted.

6. Below poverty line population, especially those who are landless and mainly depend on wage work for their unsecured livelihood may be categorized under two categories: one who most often seasonally out-migrate and engage themselves in non-agricultural activities for their income and livelihood, and two, those who stay in the village and mainly do farm wage work. Persons under category one, can take the help of village and kinship network in out-migration, searching work and accommodation at the place of destination. Increasing number of trains for distant places even from the small places, decreasing regular employment opportunity at the local level and increasing lust in favour of consumer culture and urban way of life encourage them to out-migrate. Most of these out migrants are from the lower castes. It is youth and male

dominated migration. Frequently, they send money through money order, bank draft and by hand to their family members. This money has different impact in poverty eradication depending on multiple factors including location of the family in areas like flood-prone, drought-prone, violence-prone and normal areas. This section of the population need specific treatment for their better income and saving. Before moving out, they should be provided training and orientation for at least one week at the block level, for their capacity building as well as techniques to save more and more income. Suppose a man goes to Delhi for carpentry work with having minimum training of carpentry, definitely his bargaining power will increase and subsequently the income will also increase. Also, a proper guidance should be provided to the would be migrants about the place where they wish to go or they should go? What they should do? How they should lead life? And how to cope with the anticipated or unanticipated challenges? They should also be trained to manage and spend income at their native places.

Those who do not migrate and do wage work at the native place, they need different treatment. Suppose, they are the field wage earner or rickshaw-puller, this work do not provide work in all the seasons or all days within one season. Here, attempt shall be made to associate them with two or three sources of income. All these sources of income may be primary and unorganized. All these sources may not become uneconomical and redundant at one point of time. Hence, the income will flow continuously and regularly. And income from one work will strengthen income possibility from other sources. For instance, suppose one is working as a wage earner and at the same time, he is also rickshaw-puller. In this situation, he has two sources of income. Income from wage work will help to modernize rickshaw and income from rickshaw will help to improve quality of life. The net result will be overall development. Similarly, rickshaw work will also widen social network and relationship, resulting thereby social capital formation.

Conclusion

Today, there is sufficient revenue with the government of India. However, the main source of revenue is not the primary sector like agriculture or related activities. Rather, it is the secondary sector like service which is dominantly contributing to economic growth. People at large living specially in villages have nothing to do with the secondary sector. Today, at the level of contribution in the national economy they are at the margin. They are forced now to remain at the receiving end. If we want our growing economy to sustain, it must be made inclusive. We should create an environment which may ensure participation of rural population in the development of national economy. Some of the prescriptions suggested above may be experimented as a pilot project at the district level to promote growth with peace and justice. However, we must remember that for growth to be sustainable, equal attention is required on the issues of basic health and basic education.

2

Economics and Development of Castes and Tribes

D.K. VERMA

The scheduled castes (SCs) and scheduled tribes (STs) of our country, in general, and of Madhya Pradesh, in particular, present a scenario of intrinsic complexity of disabilities and colossal magnitude of exploitation, mainly due to innate coalescence of social structured and organized economic inequalities over the centuries. The time of independence of India, was in fact the first-ever milestone in the entire history of our caste-ridden society to induct constitutional and moral responsibility to evolve an egalitarian order over a structure of graded inequality against the SCs and STs who had suffered exorabilities for centuries.

Since independence, a number of protective and promotional measures have been adopted to ensure social justice for them on the one hand, and their socio-economic development, on the other. From a state of invisibility, SCs and STs have transmogrified themselves into one of the visibility and beyond any doubt they have come a long way. There is a perceptible change in the scenario of the SCs and STs, as compared to what it was at the time of independence of our country. They have indeed undergone a conspicuous transformation. However, there is still a very wide gap between the aspirations and achievements in their development and the matter concerns much because that gap is widening and at a much faster rate than ever between scheduled and non-scheduled groups in our society. The basic question is, in spite of the political will and priority concerns shown by both the central and state governments of either political ideology during post-independent India, why and how development efforts through positive discrimination policy fail to ensure equality in all the spheres of Indian life?

These questions relate to attitude of people, social justice and development, eco-ethical concerns. The major question in sustainable development also rests upon values and attitude of people towards socio-economic and ecological order. The existing distribution of resources and income was a continued function of the past undemocratic system of deprivation to lower and privileges to higher in the social order, which simply perpetuate inequality and injustices in the society. In fact, roles of individuals or groups in our country are still mainly guided by their social status. Elites among SCs and STs are playing their roles efficiently and effectively but once they come out of the power gambit, they become totally helpless due to prevailing caste-dynamics. The present paper is in three parts and mainly attempts to analyze the caste dynamics in the economic development of SCs and STs particularly with reference to Madhya Pradesh.

I
Socio-economic Development of SCs and STs: Reflections from Madhya Pradesh Human Development Report, Bhopal Document and Mhow *Sankalp Patra*

Uneven development had always characterized the Indian situation. Madhya Pradesh had been among the most economically backward states of India. Analyzing the centre-state relations, the Government of Madhya Pradesh (HDR, 2002) emphasized that the problems of human development in the country had increasingly became problems of selected Indian states, had characteristics that were not universally shared across Indian states and needed responses that account for the specificity of those states. More than ever, human development in India had become less of an 'Indian' issue and more the issue of selected Indian states.

Both SCs and STs have been the focus of political parties, academicians and functionaries alike, mainly due to their sizeable number in the state. Besides having the largest population of *adivasis* (tribals) and a sizeable population of untouchables, Madhya Pradesh gets another distinction of having the birthplace of the great crusader of social justice and the emancipator of Indian society, Bharat Ratna Babasaheb Bhim Rao Ambedkar at Mhow (now renamed as Dr Ambedkar Nagar). Hence, a majority of leaders belonging to various national and regional level parties visit Mhow and look at Madhya Pradesh for its development programmes meant for SCs and STs.

Accordingly, the state had done some innovations and pioneering works like local self-governance through Panchayat Raj, particularly giving due advantage to SCs and STs. Similarly, inspired by the United Nations Development Report, the Government of Madhya Pradesh released first Human Development Report of any state in the country. So far, three Human Development Reports of Madhya Pradesh have been released.

The high dependency of states on the centre for funding development programmes for SCs and STs and in a situation where the statistics presented by ruling and opposition parties reveal contrasting conditions, the review of the socio-economic development of most underprivileged and sensitive groups like SCs and STs becomes a tremendous task and justice cannot be done through one paper like this one. However, an attempt is being made to reflect upon the salient features of socio-economic development of SCs and STs of Madhya Pradesh as compiled through the review of empirical studies, annual reports of the concerning departments of the government as well as reports and documents released from time to time by the ruling and opposition parties on the status of SCs and STs of Madhya Pradesh.

The First Report of Madhya Pradesh came in 1995, which benchmarked the status on human development indicators in the state. The first report led to UNDP organizing a national seminar at Bhopal coordinated by Richard Jolly, persuaded other state governments to prepare similar reports. Several state governments have since produced their respective state-level Human Development Reports.

The Second Report in 1998 highlighted changes in the human development situation. The Noble laureate and the eminent economist Prof Amartya Sen released the Second Human Development Report of Madhya Pradesh. The Government of India also released a national level Human Development Report in 2001 but six years after the first HDR of the state.

The Third Human Development Report of Madhya Pradesh was released in 2002. In that report, livelihood security was considered the utmost important challenge before the state. The agenda for the socio-economic development of Dalits was seen as a means using the power of democracy for development. However, at national level, the Planning Commission saw acceleration of growth in the nineties in seven states as reported in the Mid-Term Appraisal of Ninth Five-Year Plan.

To Quote from the Report

"Seven states showed an acceleration of growth in the 1990s. They are fairly well-distributed regionally, i.e., Gujarat (9.6%), Maharashtra (8.0%), West Bengal (6.9%), Tamil Nadu (6.2%), Madhya Pradesh (6.2%), Rajasthan (5.9%) and Kerala (5.8%)". Per capita income has also grown over the period though at a slower rate on account of slow pace of population reduction. The per capita income of Madhya Pradesh, which was Rs 6,577 in 1993–94 has gone up to Rs 7,088 in 1996–97 and Rs 7,947 by 1999–2000.

According to the National Human Development Report, 2001, headcount ratio of rural poverty went down in Madhya Pradesh from 40.6 per cent in 1993–1994 to 37.1 per cent in 1999–2000. Headcount ratio of poverty in urban areas during the same period went down from 48.4 per cent to 38.4 per cent. According to NHDR 2001, Madhya Pradesh, among the BIMARU states has the second highest HDI (Rajasthan has the highest) at 0.328 while Uttar Pradesh is at 0.314 and Bihar at 0.308.

The report also mentioned about the use of social energy for development in the form of 'Grain Bank', a common pool of grain to which all members contributed and drew according to their need and repay, and managed by communities to tide over adverse conditions in years of crop failure. Over 2,500 villages had Grain Banks managed by Self-Help Groups by the start of 2003. Formation of Self-Help Groups, where people come together for micro-finance activities, was seen as a major revival in the state from 1998 onwards.

These Self-Help Groups began as thrift and credit groups and later moved into activities of micro-credit for economic activity. They were supported through a series of government programmes like Swarna Jayanti Gramin Swarojgar Yojana, Swashakti Yojana, Swayamsidha Yojana, Indira Gandhi Garibi Hatao Yojana, etc.

The report stated the fact, that the central planning system had not been able to address the increasing gap as could be seen from the data on agreed outlays of the Tenth Plan and its comparison with Ninth Plan. States like Madhya Pradesh, Bihar, Uttar Pradesh and Rajasthan faired poorly in terms of Tenth Plan outlays (they showed negative growth compared to Ninth Plan agreed outlays) while many other states, including states with better economic and infrastructure indicators such as Andhra Pradesh, Tamil Nadu and Maharashtra, faired much better.

Reflecting upon the disadvantages arising out of the different political ideologies between centre and state, the report mentioned that external assistance, which in overall terms might constitute only 0.4 per cent of India's GNP, was skewed in favour of a few states. The Mid-Term Appraisal of the Ninth Plan by the Planning Commission admitted that seven states namely, Andhra Pradesh, Maharashtra, Uttar Pradesh, Tamil Nadu, Gujarat, Karnataka and West Bengal received more than 80 per cent of the entire external assistance.

The report considered that a sensitive reform-based funding would actually focus on softening the immediate adverse impact of reform on these states and instead the current thinking seemed to be to reward those with initial advantages on the grounds of moving faster on the reform track. While Madhya Pradesh was seen as a reforming state for such assistance, its larger case rested on the backlog in infrastructure and human development that required additional resource support. It would also not be correct to highlight inadequacies in human development without reference to the possible relation that had with the strategy of growth being pursued and its impact on the resources available for social policies. In recent years, states had been deprived of their expected share in central taxes.

The decline in central tax-GDP ratio implied that the volume of tax revenues transferred to the states was being squeezed. That was of far greater consequences to states since their ability to borrow was not as flexible as that of the centre. States were increasingly "facing a major resource crunch to sustain a reasonable social policy agenda", stated the report.

The Human Development Reports of Madhya Pradesh had been criticized for several reasons, as it was not possible to compare the indices calculated for districts in the 1995 report with those in the recent one, the income index used in the 1995 Madhya Pradesh HDI was not based solely on the UNDP formula of purchasing power parity dollar adjusted per capita income. It was based on a one time experiment in calculating district income grafted on a district's share in rural poverty and the level of deprivation of the poor.

District-level poverty ratios were also based on the results of the household survey done for the Integrated Rural Development Programme, which are generally considered to be rather unreliable. Despite major variations in the methodology for calculating HDIs between the first and second Madhya Pradesh Human Development Reports, however, it was surprising that rankings of districts against the two sets of human development indices for Madhya Pradesh had not changed during that period. On the other hand, there was substantial overall improvement in the range of variation in district-level indices, where the earlier range between the best and worst districts was between 0.619 and 0.156 (a difference of 46.3 basis points), it was then between 0.637 and 0.356 (a difference of only 28.1 basis points).

Nevertheless, the greater importance of the Human Development Report lies in the recognition that disparities in Madhya Pradesh and in that sense in India too, were not merely a class or gender dimension but also a caste and tribe dimension. Hence, the report suggested developing in India, like the UNDP did the Gender Development Index in 1995, a Scheduled Tribe-Scheduled Caste Development Index to capture the inequality in opportunities to human development faced by the people belonging to the scheduled castes and scheduled tribes.

The Bhopal Document: Charting a New Course for Dalits for 21st Century

The Government of Madhya Pradesh prepared the Bhopal Document (January 2002). The Document was circulated at the Bhopal Conference, January 12–13, 2002 where the Bhopal Declaration was adopted. The opening sentence of the Bhopal Document stated that it was an attempt by the government to put forward an unexpurgated agenda and invite a free and frank debate on the future of 250 million *adivasis* and untouchables of the country. The Document incorporated various national and international reports and information including that of the US, South Africa, besides Madhya Pradesh.

The document included the Bhopal Declaration also, which was adopted unanimously by the Bhopal conference and demanded 21-point action agenda for the 21st century. The chapter four in the first section discussed the economic profile of Dalits. It mentioned that the majority of SCs and STs were in the primary sector, where the per capita labour and circulation of currency were lowest. The further categorization of primary sector workforce into cultivators and landless labourers revealed the grater incidence of landless labourers among SCs followed by STs. Of the landholdings, 86.6 per cent among SCs and 64.8 per cent among STs was small and marginal with poor irrigation facilities.

Thus, SCs and STs were highly marginalized. Accordingly, the MP model of development was planned to be mainly guided by the assumption that unless land-labour relationships in the country was recognized, no amount of activism on the part of the state could liberate SCs and STs from their existing condition and continued landlessness among them would be major obstacle in the social democracy, the core of Ambedkar's philosophy.

The document emphasized upon the prioritized land reforms and restoration of tribal land besides food security, grain bank and empowering cultivators. On March 4, 1998, the state government issued order to all district collectors to reduce the Charnoi (grazing) land area from 7.5 per cent to 5 per cent, 2.5 per cent of the Charnoi land so spared was distributed among SCs and STs.

The Charnoi land of 5 per cent was further reduced to 2 per cent in September 2001 and the 3 per cent land so recovered was redistributed among SCs and STs. Thus, in the phase I, 1.54 lakh acres of land and in phase II, 6 lakh acres of land, a total of 7.54 lakh acres of land (market value Rs 3,750 crore) was redistributed to about 4 lakh of SC and ST families (more than 15% of the total landless agricultural labourers 26.06 lakh including 11.42 lakh SCs and 14.64 lakh STs) in Madhya Pradesh.

The Bhopal Document and the Bhopal Conference tried to consolidate SCs and STs under one umbrella, Dalits. The MP model of economic development considered the indicator, the rate workers' shift away from the primary to two other sectors, a very crucial one.

Mhow *Sankalp Patra*

The then opposition political party in Madhya Pradesh organized a two-day *Dalit Sammelan* on April 25–26, 2003 at Mhow. During the inauguration of the Sammelan, Mhow *Sankalp Patra* prepared by the state scheduled castes wing of the party was released by the party's national president. The concept paper of the *Dalit Sammelan* criticized the policies and programmes being implemented by the then ruling party for the upliftment of the scheduled castes.

It stated that the constitutional provisions in favour of Dalits were not being implemented in their right and proper perspective and hence, the socio-economic and political status of Dalits in the state was poor and in fact had deteriorated during last ten years (1992–2002). Atrocities on Dalits particularly against women were on increase. The state had become the second in the country in case of rape cases on Dalit women and stood on the third place with regard to the atrocities on Dalits.

The participation of Dalits in the property holding and productive assets was almost negligible. The disparities between the Dalits and other groups had widened. The rural population of Dalits had suffered badly as most of them were the landless labourers. In the urban areas also their condition was bad as many of them were poor and living on menial and low-paid jobs. The participation of Dalits had decreased in the Jawahar Rojgar Yojana while their participation in the scheme had increased at national level.

The land redistribution was seen as a statistical play and was infusing class struggle, as a larger position of the distributed land was either encroached or was already in possession of Dalits or other weaker sections of the society. The employment scenario was not conducive for Dalits as there were 8,023 backlog vacancies while there were only 3,554 posts available. During 1993–2002, the amount received by the state for welfare programmes and schemes of Dalits was not properly utilized as out of Rs 239.49 crore received only Rs 196.74 crore was spent.

The direction set in the *Sankalp Patra* was towards social harmony, empowerment and all-round development of scheduled classes and the Sankalp was dedicated to SCs. Ideals of inspirers like Mahatma Gandhi, Bhim Rao Ambedkar, Sant Ravidas, Mahatma Jyotiba Phuley and Deen Dayal Upadhyaya were said to be incorporated in schemes to be formulated for the upliftment of SCs. The aim declared was to ensure social dignity to scheduled castes, their economic upliftment and participation in power. The *Sankalp Patra* requested the central government to take actions on 23 points raised therein and made 11 specific recommendations including schemes for local employment, special provisions for migratory labours, distribute 5 acres of land to all landless labourers and Rs 1,000 per acre as grant, link education and employment to increase opportunities for self-employment and to encourage entrepreneurship among SCs making them capable in the competitive economy.

The party made a declaration that Madhya Pradesh would be developed as a Model State for Dalits. The Mhow *Sankalp Patra* discussed mainly the problems of SCs and STs.

II

Caste Economics: Empirical Studies on Socio-economic Development of SCs and STs of Madhya Pradesh

Economists have recognized the problems of inequality associated with the caste system. However, empirical studies and theoretical understanding on caste-based intricacies in relation to economic development are not only scarce but diverse too. Deshpande and Thorat (2000) reviewed three main types of approaches including mainstream classical, Marxian and Ambedkar's approaches on the caste-economics. The classical approach relied on the fact that in Indian society, occupation or economic activities were hereditary, compulsory and endogenous. Marxian approach attributed caste-based exploitative relations mainly to the economic forces.

Ambedkar (1987) viewed Hindu social system as a framework of production organization and also a scheme of distribution involving hereditary and fixed occupations, unequal ownership rights and penalties, if the system was broken or not maintained. No economic rights to untouchables and multiple privileges and rights to upper castes particularly, Brahmins were the governing principles of caste-based inequality and that graded inequality lead to the division of labourers (Ambedkar, 1979).

The caste-based discrimination in so far as it excluded or reduced the access of SCs and STs persons to various economic factors like markets, labour, land, capital, information and service sector, had implications on their earning capacities, employment and income ultimately affecting their standard of living and quality of life.

The statistics on landownership, employment wages and credits provided concrete evidences of caste-based discrimination against SCs and STs (Thorat, 1998). Thus, indication and consequences of caste-based discrimination in economics are beyond doubt. In that regard, the scenario of economic development of SCs and STs of Madhya Pradesh is being discussed taking help from the empirical studies.

These studies were conducted in the form of various projects at Dr Babasaheb Ambedkar National Institute of Social Sciences, Mhow, on various aspects including concerns on the economic development of SCs and STs of Madhya Pradesh. The studies confirm the fact that even after celebrating the golden jubilee of independence and as a democratic, republic and socialist nation, and also establishing a framework for egalitarian social order as envisaged in the Constitution of India, and further extending the local self-governance at the village level through Panchayat Raj in Madhya Pradesh, caste-based socio-economic disabilities and discrimination continue their multifarious forms in our society.

Compilation of such studies (Verma and Sohrot, 2003) reveals the status of economic development, and bottlenecks and obstacles in the development of scheduled castes and scheduled tribes of Madhya Pradesh.

Atrocities, Disabilities and Segregation

The major obstacle in sustaining the economic development of scheduled castes and scheduled tribes is the reaction by the non-scheduled groups, which is usually reflected in the form of atrocities and continuation of traditional disabilities imposed against them. Interviewing 237 victims from Ujjain, Guna, Morena, Satna, Shajapur and Indore districts, Singh (1997) found that atrocities varied from heinous crimes like murder and rape to physical torture, sexual assault and discrimination especially in order to sustain centuries old disabilities on SCs. Poor and landless laboureres were more vulnerable. In 23 per cent cases, dispute over land and in more than 18 per cent cases, dispute over wages, repayment of debt and terms and conditions of semi-bonded labour were the main causes of atrocities. In another study in the village Kolukhedi, district Bhopal, it was found that the SCs in rural areas were as much economically exploited by the dominant section of non-Hindu communities as by the Hindu communities. That means the majority of the cases of atrocities (41%) resulted from the process of economic development of SCs and there is a changing dynamics extending the caste-Hindu-based economic exploitation to non-Hindu class.

In a study on degree of untouchability in 34 villages of Mhow tehsil, district Indore, Naik (1999) observed that most of the respondents wanted to get rid of their traditional occupations like beggary, working in hide, carrying corpses, rearing of pigs, beating drums, delivering messages, cleansing, etc. But non-scheduled groups compelled them to continue those jobs as alternatives provided to them by the government were rendered unviable and were intentionally made non-feasible by keeping no economic relations with them. Their wage earning rates were as low as Rs 12 to Rs 25 per day. The untouchable labourers especially women were compelled to work for a longer time on the farms of the *Savarnas.* Even labourers of the same economic status but belonging to other than SCs, also disliked to work with labourers belonging to scheduled castes.

Verma and Joshi (2000) in a study on social segregation in 18 villages from six cultural zones of the Madhya Pradesh, found a distinct pattern of the SCs *bastis,* which were usually on least favoured terrain and downward locations and had comparatively lower level of infrastructure and problems, aggravated further with poor accessibility to even that low infrastructure, resources and amenities mainly due to economic disabilities imposed by the non-scheduled groups which somehow did not allow sale of land possessed by them to scheduled castes.

The study also showed that the economic and political empowerment of SCs was not leading to their social empowerment, as in spite of recognizing their economic and political upliftment, the non-scheduled groups were not ready to give social respect and dignity to scheduled groups. The main reason found during the discussion with the villagers, was the continued faith in the religious books and holy scriptures, which instead of the Constitution of India, still guide the social order. Simply, the people were not aware about the constitutional provisions and so far no attempt was made to make them aware and informed about the changes that have been made through the Constitution of India restructuring traditional social order into an egalitarian one.

Scavenging in Madhya Pradesh

Gadkar (1998) in a study on 206 scavengers families in Indore city found that illiterates as compared to the literates, the less educated compared to the more educated, and the women compared to men were all, by and large, still attached to caste-bound scavenging occupation. One of the most striking features of the change that had taken place among them was in the *jagirdari* system (hereditary customary right) attached to the scavenging occupation. About 82 per cent grandfathers, 63 per cent of the fathers (heads of families) and only 30 per cent of the present generation were following the traditional *jagirdari* system.

In another study on scavengers in Bhind, Jabalpur and Indore districts, Singh (2000) observed that there were more than 7 lakh households using service latrines in the state out of which a little more than 6 lakh were in the urban areas. The maximum population of scavengers was found in Bhind district, followed by Jabalpur and Indore districts. The scavengers cleaned the bucket privies of the households both independently or on the *jagirdari* basis. Besides, they were employed on regular or part-time basis in corporations, municipalities, cantonment boards, government and semi-government offices, mills and factories, schools, hospitals, theatres and housing societies and complexes. The supply of equipment (hand gloves, gumboots, sprangers, hand carts, wheel barrows, etc.) to scavengers had been inadequate and that too were hardly used.

Under the National Scheme for Liberation and Rehabilitation of Scavengers and their Dependents, 4,695 scavengers were trained during 1992–93 to 1998–99 in Madhya Pradesh and an amount of Rs

1,542.205 lakh was spent for this purpose. Moreover, 69,751 scavengers were rehabilitated and an amount of Rs 7,279.76 lakh was spent on their rehabilitation. The Sulabh International had constructed more than 10 lakh flush water seal latrines in Madhya Pradesh between 1989–90 and 1997–98. Consequently, the percentage of sweepers engaged in scavenging declined. But, the fact remains that service latrines still existed and the practice of manual scavenging continued in the state, though it was confined to pockets especially in the suburbs of the cities and the very congested central places of small towns.

It was reported in the study that the scavengers in Madhya Pradesh belonged to 42 SCs communities. However, prominent among them were the Bhangi, the Dom and the Ghasiya castes. The Doms were relatively more urban-based while the Ghasiyas were predominantly rural-based and tradition bound. The Helals or the Helalkhores among the Muslims particularly in Ujjain also performed the task of scavenging on a traditional basis.

There was a distinct trend towards both inter-generational and intra-generational occupational mobility among the scavengers in the Madhya Pradesh, however, horizontal mobility was more prominent among them. The non-availability of sanitary toilet facility to the people at large (nearly 70%) and continuance of the obnoxious practice of manual scavenging in the country, howsoever marginal it may be, confirmed that in spite of the sincere and honest efforts of the government and the people during more than fifty years of independence, the abominable practice could not be abolished from the root and branch.

Livelihood Options and Labour Migration

In a study on tribal migration from 66 villages of Jhabua district, Joshi (1994) found that nearly 97 per cent of them were cultivators but the contribution of agriculture produce to the total family income was 32.6 per cent only. The livestock contributed 7.9 per cent and the income from forest produce was as low as 1.1 per cent. Nearly 53 per cent of the family workers, besides cultivating their own fields, also worked as labourers. The wages earned as labourers were the main source (54.7%) of family income. The quantum of the seasonal migration was very large. On an average 46.3 per cent of the tribal population migrated out and that went as high as 70 per cent in some parts of Jhabua.

Although in the drought years the migration was on a larger scale, in the normal years too, the migration was not less than 43 per cent. The season of migration was from October to June. The tribals migrated in all directions, especially to the urban centres of Kota, Surat, Vadodara, Ahmedabad, Indore, Bhopal and Dahod. The migration from Jhabua was a part of the strategy for survival and therefore was not selective with reference to age, sex and marital status.

Barring very old people, all the family members migrated out. Small children also accompanied their mothers. The level of skill in the workforce was extremely low. The percentage of skilled workers was merely one. Nearly all the migrants were unskilled workers and 80 per cent of them were engaged in construction activities followed by agricultural operations and working in brick kilns or quarries rank.

Joshi and Verma studied sustainable livelihood options and labour migration from 100 villages of 90 development blocks in 5 districts, viz., Rajnandgaon, Durg, Raipur, Bilaspur and Raigarh of the Chhattisgarh region of undivided Madhya Pradesh. A special nature of the economy in the region was noticed where migrate in offseason had not only become a compulsion but also an important economic asset for the scheduled castes and scheduled tribes. In spite of the agriculture being the main economic activity of 69 per cent of the households, to migrate out in search of livelihood options became necessary as the income from agriculture was very low due to very small land holdings, and a vast majority of them were landless labourers besides, innovations in their traditional agricultural practices were almost nil.

A high degree of caste selectivity was also noted in the migration. A large percentage of the scheduled castes were either marginal farmers or landless labourers and these were the categories from which maximum migration occurred. The scheduled tribes whose share in the population was much higher than the scheduled castes, had lower propensity to migrate.

The pull factors were the coinciding of the peak work season in construction and brick-making with the off-farm season in Chhattisgarh, large demand for workers resulting in easy availability of work, attractive wages as compared to that available in farm sector at home, possibility of earning more in work-based contractual work, possibility of employment of the entire family at one place, attraction of advance payment, free travel, preference for Chhattisgarh workers as compared to local workers due to various reasons, some attraction for city life, especially among young persons, and the absence of any psychological barrier or social stigma for those who migrate.

Tribal Economy in Madhya Pradesh

A study on tribals and panchayats in 27 villages of Jhabua and Bastar districts by Maurya (1996) emphasized that the Panchayat Raj had yet to address the basic issues of poverty, unemployment and exploitation of tribal resources. The tribals had become subservient in their places of domination due to the intervention and exploitation of vested interests, i.e., non-tribals who were so powerful in deciding the direction of tribal policy and economy overtly and covertly at the grassroots level of tribal setting.

The developmental infrastructure in tribal-dominated districts of Bastar and Jhabua was very poor and was not able to meet the rising needs and aspirations of the tribals. As far as the economic development was concerned, the tribals had welcomed the new Panchayat Raj. However, the problems of coordination and cooperation between officials and Panchayat Raj representatives were posing a serious challenge for the effective functioning of new Panchayat Raj Institutions.

Joshi (1998), studying economic impact of water scarcity problems in 24 villages of Jhabua district, found that most of the respondents worked as labourers along with cultivating their own land, which was largely unirrigated. The size of family had become more than double as compared to what it was at grandfather's time, while the land holding had remained the same. The dependency on land for livelihood had decreased, while the share of income earned through wages by working out of Jhabua had increased considerably.

In a census data-based study on the Baiga primitive tribe group conducted in 40 villages in Shahdol, Sidhi, Mandla, Balaghat, Surguja, Bilaspur and Rajnandgaon districts by Joshi and Verma revealed the fact that the ratio of working population among the Baiga was significantly higher and the participation of female in work was found more than twice the general population. More than

95 per cent of both the main and the marginal workers were engaged in primary production or were working as labourers.

However, the inter-generational occupational mobility in the Baigas depicted a negative trend in which more and more farmers were compelled to leave farming and to join the workforce as unskilled labourers. The skill element in the Baiga workers was more or less missing even in the existing generation while comparatively in other communities, the skill component had increased perceptibly.

A sizable share of agricultural land cultivated by the Baigas was acquired through encroachment of forest land. Nearly 90 per cent of the Baiga farmers did not have any source of irrigation. Joshi (1992), in a study of Indore, Dhar, Dewas, Ujjain, Shajapur, Mandsaur, Ratlam and Jhabua districts, also showed that innovations did not take place in the traditional techniques among scheduled tribes.

The above references make it clear that the tribal economy in Madhya Pradesh has remained more or less in the same state as it used to be at the time of independence and the major lacuna could be identified as almost negligible upgradation in their skills and lack of innovations in their indigenous and traditional technologies.

Impact of Policies and Programmes

Nagendra Ambedkar (1992) in an evaluation study of IRDP in Jabera block, Damoh district, found that contrary to the guidelines, a number of the non-poor, i.e., those whose income was well above the poverty line, were assisted in a greater number. There was an overwhelming bias towards animal husbandry schemes, especially milk cattle for which beneficiaries were not trained and thus, the beneficiaries could not generate the desired income. Joshi (1992) studied the impact of Tendu Patta Policy in 15 villages of Indore, Dewas, Raisen, Sagar, Mandla and Bilaspur districts and found that functionally the policy had resulted into the bureaucratization of the trade. The cooperative societies, though involved the target groups mainly the tribals, could not handle the trade independently due to lack of training. The increase in wages had been ineffective due to decreased plucking days and the increased cost of living. Studies on post-matric scholarship schemes also reflected upon disadvantages of income ceilings. Joshi (1994) in a study conducted in Raigarh and Indore districts found that out of the total eight per cent of the students, who were not getting the scholarship due to different reasons, nearly half of them were due to the restriction of the income ceiling clause. Being in service was the second important reason for not getting the scholarship. The effect of the income-ceiling clause had been found comparatively more pronounce in the case of girl students. Besides, a majority of the students were not able to cover even 25 per cent of their cost of living from the existing maintenance allowance.

In an another study on the scheme covering 1,500 beneficiaries including 801 SCs and 699 STs in Jhabua, Ujjain and Indore districts, Verma (1999) found that only 8 per cent respondents were having family income above Rs 60,000 and a majority of their parents belonged to the service sector. The study also showed that the effect of the differential income ceiling, i.e., provision of half of the maintenance allowance was negligible for non-service families. The two-tier system mainly affected the service sector, the reason being that they need to produce income certificate from the employer. The two-tier system of income ceiling was not inducing any perceptible impact except on salaried families. Rather, it tended to leave the scope for manipulation by the rest of the occupational categories to manage the income certificates below the maximum income ceiling so as to become eligible for the scholarship. Thus, the needy among scheduled castes and scheduled tribes were deprived of their genuine need.

Similarly, in the resource generation sector also policies and programmes need reorientation and effective monitoring as Verma (1997) in a study on social forestry in the Indore social forestry range emphasized that availability and accessibility to resources, particularly the forest-based resources were the crucial factors disturbing the expenditure pattern of the weaker sections, as they used to get such needs fulfilled without any cost from the nearby forest areas.

The study showed that 84 per cent of the beneficiaries belonged to SCs and STs and 78 per cent among them were landless. However, the low survival rate of the plantation and the improper selection of the species planted (eucalyptus, 75%), compounded by lack of training and guidance, insecurity of plantation and water scarcity, defeated the purpose and adversely affected expected benefits intended from the scheme.

Thus, the scheme was found successful only at the level of selecting the beneficiaries, but failed miserably in maintaining and ensuring the benefits to the target groups. The economically marginalized sections get further marginalized through such approaches. Maurya (1998) in a study on Special Component Plan (SCP) conducted in Gwalior, Ujjain, Raipur and Bilaspur districts covering rural development and forestry programme found that 36 per cent of them were landless labourers.

Most of the landowners were small and marginal farmers. SC beneficiaries were discriminated in labour market also. Even under the SCP income generating scheme, they did not get preference in employment and there was an overwhelming majority (93%) of beneficiaries who were exploited by officials and contractors alike, who denied them minimum wages in forestry schemes.

In a comparative study of the Scheduled Castes Financial Development Corporation (SCFDC) programmes in Madhya Pradesh and Andhra Pradesh, Maurya (2002) found that the Andhra Pradesh SCFDC, established in 1974, was well-organized in terms of its administrative structure from state to grassroots level. The roles and functions of its different administrative wings were well-defined and very innovative in nature as compared to that of the SCFDC set up in Madhya Pradesh in 1979.

However, the Andhra Pradesh Scheduled Caste Financial Development Corporation was not able to eradicate fully the cumulative deprivation of the scheduled castes because of the challenges of the market forces and the hostile role of dominant castes who were neutralizing the fuller impact of its development effort.

Caste-Gender Economics: Economic Status of SCs and STs Women in Madhya Pradesh

The economic status of women particularly of SCs and STs in Madhya Pradesh was found very low and little change had occurred in their economic development since independence. Sharma (1998), in a study on Bedia women inhabiting Sukha and Pathari villages of Raisen, found that women were the head of the household.

The girls got into the traditional profession of flesh trade and male members just did nothing. The Bedias of Sukha Karar were poor and their living condition was pitiable. Men could be seen loitering around or sitting under the tree, playing cards and smoking. Children were normally either playing in the ground or serving the clients by bringing liquor, cigarettes or pan for them. The girls of 10–13 age group were all prepared to take up their position in the trade. The Bedias themselves were not hesitant in accepting prostitution as a profession and so there was no need to either hide it or feel ashamed about it. The same was true about men, women and even children also. The children talk very casually about customers and they also try to make the customers comfortable in every respect.

In an another study assessing the economic status of women among the SCs and STs in Morena, Harda, Damoh, Shajapur, Sheopur, Neemach and Sagar districts, Sharma (2001) found that in rural areas the annual family income of 31.7 per cent families of SCs and 31.4 per cent of STs was below or up to Rs 12,000 while in urban areas it was 6.6 per cent and 3.4 per cent among SCs and STs respectively.

In rural areas, 84 per cent of SC women and 89 per cent of ST women were marginal workers, while in urban areas 77 per cent and 82 per cent of them respectively, were marginal workers. Similarly, 82.5 per cent among the SCs and 55 per cent of among the STs in rural areas contributed to the family income directly. Both SCs and STs in majority of the cases borrowed money for livelihood problems.

Both in rural areas and urban areas, neither the SC nor the ST women were getting equal wages for equal work in unorganized sectors. In another study on the female infanticide in the Chambal division, Sharma (2001) reported that sex ratio was less than 700. The study showed that the first-born girl child had high percentage of chances of survival in comparison to the second and the third born girls mainly due to economic compulsions.

The above review of empirical studies reflecting upon the scenario with regard to the socio-economic status of SCs and STs of Madhya Pradesh clearly establish caste-based discrimination and disabilities. The benefits being provided by the state are not being utilized in their full potential by the SCs and STs mainly due to resistance from the non-scheduled groups. The schemes and programmes of the state have become the idle target achievements. Though, the scheduled castes and scheduled tribes have become politically aware of their status and privileges but the social system is not providing them a proper platform to reap the benefits. The economic empowerment of scheduled groups is also not being supported by the society to trickle down the benefits in their social interests of dignity and harmony.

Therefore, it could be concluded that in a caste-ridden society like ours, merely target achievements and considering the SCs and STs as the passive beneficiaries would not sustain their socio-economic development. The above empirical analysis of the socio-economic development of SCs and STs of Madhya Pradesh during the post-independent period, place the following points for consideration:

1. In spite of the sincere efforts and political will, the socio-economic development of SCs and STs of Madhya Pradesh was not leading to their social empowerment, particularly to enhance capabilities to enjoy equality in all spheres of human life, which is, in fact the greater aim of their economic development.
2. Land redistribution to SCs and STs of Madhya Pradesh was not made following the philosophy of Ambedkar, particularly with regard to small holdings and collective farming, hence the benefits accrued become doubtful from sustainable development perspective.
3. The development of SCs and STs had become more a political agenda with government (either political party of any ideology) rather than giving priority to or serve their socio-economic interests.
4. The gap between aspirations or achievements of SCs and STs had widened during the post-independent period, mainly due to target orientation in the socio-economic development of SCs and STs, since such kind of approach was not designed to sustain accrued benefits to them.
5. Redistribution of productive assets in favour of SCs and STs had resulted in their further marginalization and had made them more vulnerable as the cases of atrocities particularly with regard to land ownership had increased substantially during the

last five years. In other words, caste dynamics in socio-economic development was playing a greater role than ever.

6. The funds made available for various schemes for the economic development of SCs and STs were not fully utilized and a larger part of that remained unspent, leaving wide gaps in the target achievements.
7. Economic exploitation of SCs and STs continued and except a small change in employment sector, particularly in the government service, their economic status had not changed much from what it was at the time of independence.
8. Large-scale migration of SCs and STs in search of livelihood from resource scarce region had become a regular phenomenon. Incident, magnitude and extent of labour migration had gradually increased over the last five decades of independence.
9. SCs and STs were discriminated in markets and wages. They were paid low as compared to the minimum wages and also their goods were not supported with proper exchange rates and readily accepted by the mainstream of the society. Only SCs/STs preferred to take tea and snacks from the restaurants run by scheduled castes in villages of Madhya Pradesh. While, in urban areas such discrimination was not seen mainly due to undisclosed identity of owner or servants of the restaurant.
10. Even well-off families among SCs and STs were not able to purchase land of their choice in the areas inhabited or belonging to caste-Hindus.
11. Scavenging, the most heinous type of service remained traditionally bound occupation and families belonging to particular castes were compelled to remain in the scavenging profession as the other alternatives provided to them by the government were not encouraged or accepted by the non-scheduled groups who did not maintain economic relations with them.
12. Socio-economic status of women, particularly those belonging to SCs and STs, were very low and they faced gender discrimination on a large scale.
13. The poor economic condition added another dimension to the inhuman practice of female infanticide in Madhya Pradesh, particularly in the northern part of the state.

14. Panchayat Raj had opened innovative and sustainable alternatives for SCs and STs and in the form of local self-governance, these deprived sections of the society had been given due participation.
15. However, lack of training and non-participation shown by the functionaries and the mainstream of the society were the major concerns in unsustainability of economic benefits accrued to scheduled castes and scheduled tribes.
16. Besides inviting participation of non-scheduled groups, awareness, training, skill upgradation and innovations in their indigenous and traditional technologies could be identified and made the priority in the economic development of scheduled castes and scheduled tribes of Madhya Pradesh.

In other words, the above analysis reveals that the strategies and approaches towards socio-economic development of SCs and STs of Madhya Pradesh failed to restructure social order in favour of deprived, discriminated, segregated and exploited sections of the society. Therefore, socio-economic benefits accrued to them during the post-independent period could not be sustained for the society at large.

III
Caste Dynamics and Sustainable Development

The caste dynamics has been largely ignored in planning for the socio-economic development of SCs and STs of Madhya Pradesh and at the national as well. In fact, roles of individuals or groups in our country are still mainly guided by their social status. Elites among SCs and STs of Madhya Pradesh are playing their roles efficiently and effectively but once they come out of the power gambit or support of the state is withdrawn, they become helpless. That means, the capability acquired by them remained active till they get support from the empowering agency.

In other words, the achieved status of SCs and STs through positive discrimination policy of the state is not sustainable if not supported by their capabilities. The trickle down of the economic benefits or their encashment to elevate social status, as envisaged through planning in India, thus appears a difficult target.

It is considered appropriate at this juncture to realize that the politically supported status of SCs and STs may not lead to their sustainable development, which basically means meeting the needs of the present generation without compromising the ability of the future generations to meet their own need (World Conservation Strategy, 1987). The present economic development approach is making efforts to provide needs to the present generation of SCs and STs but not ensuring their ability to meet the same in future, which is the most crucial dimension and prerequisite of sustainable development.

The problems of inequality and injustice are the major obstacles on the path of sustainable development. Sustainable development in socio-economic perspective, particularly of SCs and STs, needs to be conceptualized (Verma, 1998) as a progressive diminution in discrimination (asymmetry of social relations), exploitation (asymmetry of economic relations), deprivation (asymmetry of distribution and consumption of resources) and oppression (asymmetry of power).

Traditionally, economics was concerned with the production and allocation of goods and services and their consequent impact on the material well-being. The focus of the economic development was uncompromising on growth of incomes. Economic development in a broad sense compromised all works on the growth of incomes per head including tha of the classical economist theorists from Smith to Mills, as they saw income as one of the several but different means to important ends. Economic development or development of a region connoted such changes in economic life as were not forced upon that from without but arose from its own initiation from within.

It connoted for primarily in analyzing the existing resources in a different way, in doing new things with them, regardless of whether those resources increased or not. That also represented a disruption of the familiar and traditional process of stationery circulation arousing resistance and hurting established interests.

Being an innovative process, leading to the structural transformation of the social system, quantitative improvement in economy would lead to qualitative improvement in the society was, thus the major focus. John Mayrad Keynes, one of the most influential economists of the last century once suggested that economics would become redundant in the long run because it would solve the major problems confronting the economy.

Thereafter, many shifts have occurred in the understanding of economics as a social science helping the process of development, particularly the sustainable development. The concept of capability and the expansion of human capabilities considered as the central feature of process of such development and the economic development was thus seen in terms of expansion of opportunities that the individuals in the society enjoy (Dreze and Sen, 1999).

Economic development thus became a broad prospective that included central roles of social as well as economic opportunities offered facilities important as they were by well functioning markets and beneficial exchanges but also the fundamental role of human capabilities and their dependence on basic education, health services, ownership patterns, social stratification, gender relations and the opportunity of social cooperation as well as political protest and opposition.

Variations in social opportunities were considered leading to diverse achievements in the quality of life and the standard of living, but also influencing economic performance and in particular the citizen's could use the extent to which the facilities offered by markets in general. The main obstacle to economic development thus, could be seen as the failure of public policies to remove social inequalities.

Interestingly, Agrawal (2001) drew the attention on the debate between the economics and other social sciences and discussed some misconceptions among economists and non-economists both, on the methodological issues particularly, quantitative emphasis in the former and qualitative approach of the later. That methodological divide was more evident in the Indian social sciences as compared to the west. It was referred to an attempt that combined quantitative and qualitative approaches in poverty analysis in two recent issues of *American Journal of Political Science*, in which over one-third articles used mathematical modelling.

Those are few opinions, the first one, that the economics seen as a panacea and then the importance of capability and lastly the debate on the quantification as a methodological issue need some careful observations in Indian context, particularly with regard to scheduled castes and scheduled tribes. The main difference between India and other countries (western) lies in caste and class structure. The class economics is largely open while caste economics is latently closed, one in which economic consequences are mainly of non-economic nature. That could be the possible answer to the questions with regard to sustainable development as raised above. And, the answer would invite an analysis of the policy and programmes undertaken in the caste-ridden societies like ours.

The main thrusts of the five-year plans in our country were the growth, modernization, self-reliance and social justice. Central elements in socio-economic development strategy of the plan were generating productive employment through increase in cropping intensity, extension of agricultural technologies to the low productive regions and to small farmers, making rural development programmes more effective in creating productive assets, expansion of labour intensive construction activities for providing housing, amenities, infrastructure, expansion of primary education and health facilities and change in the pattern of industrial growth.

The central objective of the First Five-Year Plan in India was to initiate a process of development, which would raise living standard and open out to the people new opportunities for a richer and more varied life. The urge to economic and social change came from the fact of poverty and of inequalities in income, wealth and opportunities. Maximum production, full employment and the attainment of economic equality and social justice, thus, became the accepted objectives of the planning for the economic development. However, it was clearly perceived that the pace of economic development would depend on variety of factors that constitute the psychological and sociological settings within which the economy operates and hence, it was also clearly realized that for that transformation, state would have to play the crucial role.

The Second Five-Year Plan regarded the achievements of the First Five-Year Plan as no more than a beginning. To strengthen the focus, socio-economic development planning was summed up in a phrase *socialist pattern of society,* not private profit but social gain or purpose. Thereafter, successive plans strengthened economic development. However, the Sixth Plan became important in emphasizing upon thrust on the distributive justice. The economic reforms after 1991 opened up Indian economy and broadened the reach of the markets becoming more a class economy rather than caste economy but largely ignored the continuation of caste economics.

There occurred a shift in the policy and programmes after 1990s. The late 1990s was also inferred as a major disillusionment with the state as an economic agent, mainly because of the 'conditionality' sought by the IMF, the World Bank, etc. Several debates have been set on the advantages and disadvantages from the processes like globalization, liberalization and privatization to Indian society in general and SCs and STs in particular. However, irrespective of their polarized ideologies, both the major political parties of the country have agreed on the agenda of new economic reforms.

The former Minister of Commerce, Government of India, Swamy (2000) remarked that the new economic reforms of 1991–96 and its basic continuation since then by the United Front and then by National Democratic Alliance during 1997–2000 and current UPA had suffered from some major structural flaws. It was emphasized that the annual union budget had been mechanically designed to meet arbitrarily set IMF-WB target for fiscal deficit; globalization measures adopted by the government failed to recognize the internal priorities; the reforms fundamentally flawed in being introduced first in industry and not in agricultural sector.

More importantly than the agriculture, caste should have been recognized as the crucial dimension of the Indian economy. Ambedkar had much clear and most relevant vision in that regard. His vision was more close to what environmental economics conceptualize today (Verma, 1998).

Ambedkar regarded biomass production activity as primary industry. It is important to note that the primary production activities make the base for sustainable development. According to Ambedkar (1979) primary industries, i.e., those related to agricultural practices were concerned with extracting useful materials from the earth, the soil and the water. He considered primary industries important because they extract from the physical world useful materials (resources) that become the original sources of human subsistence and provide raw materials for the secondary industries.

Therefore, it is appropriate that the priorities of new economic reforms should have been on the primary industries. Ambedkar analyzed similarities and dissimilarities between fiscal and monetary problems, particularly during 1833–1919 (Nanchariah, 1997) and those were still relevant when in 1991, economic crisis and subsequent policy changes in the fiscal monetary management in India are compared. Thus, our country definitely needed economic reforms but not at the cost of the concept of welfare state. Economic reforms were considered in isolation, but that would have been meaningful only, if the weaker sections of our society were given proper and full social security due to importance of caste in Indian economics (Verma, 2000).

International financial institutions were also aware that India suffered severe deprivation in education and health, the two most important and basic structures of sound economy, particularly in the northern part of India where caste, class and gender inequalities were more pronounced. It was emphasized that economic inequalities reinforced by social barriers made it especially difficult for poor people to move out of poverty (World Bank, 1999). In the past, the poverty eradication in India lagged behind East Asia because of slower growth and significantly less progress in promoting mass education and basic health.

Caste is the biggest barrier in exchange which is the essence of economy and asset is an entity possessing market or exchange value and forming part of the wealth or property of the owner. Taking a specific example of land reforms, the caste-economics would become clearer. Land is such an important asset with the scheduled castes and scheduled tribes that for their next coming generations quality and productivity of land can largely ensure their sustainable development. However, the present land reform policies are not only erroneous but also unsustainable for scheduled castes and scheduled tribes.

There is no agreement on what constitutes land reforms, mentioned Appu (1996), who worked as the Land Reform Commissioner with the Government of India during 1970–75 and again in 1978–79. *Encyclopaedia Britannica* defined land reforms "a specified integrated action programme to bring about more effective control and use of land for the direct benefit of the agricultural purpose and for the direct benefit of the committee as a whole".

In our Constitution, land reform is a subject at the entry number 18 of the state list where it is mentioned as "land that is to say rights in or over land, land tenures including the relations of landlord and tenant, and the collection of rents, transfer and alienation of agricultural land, land improvement and the loans". The constitutional basis for Government of India's role in land reforms is emphasized at the entry number 20 of the concurrent list.

Thus, land reform has both a narrow and a broader connotation. The principal measures of land reforms opted to secure the objective of land policy laid down in five-year plans were aberration of intermediary interests, tenancy reform and ceilings on agricultural holdings. The main emphasis of land reforms was on two aspects, firstly redistribution of land in favour of landless or marginal and small cultivators, and secondly the tenancy reforms. On the eve of the independence, the area under tenancy was around one-fifth of the total area and the tenant households around one-third of the total rural household. The first immediate step taken was to check the involvement of intermediaries.

Land increase was expected to increase employment in agriculture because small holdings systematically employ more labour per hectare than large holdings. The Reserve Bank of India took a note of concentration ratio of assets; mainly agricultural land owned by the rural households that were 0.65 per cent in 1961–62 which increased by 10 per cent to 0.66 per cent in 1971–72.

The poorest 10 per cent rural household among the total rural population of the country owned only 0.1 per cent of the total land while the 10 per cent of richest owned more than half of the land in 1971–72. Out of 5.35 million acre of land estimated surplus in March-April, 1978 about 23 per cent (1.46 million acre) was distributed and about one-half accrued to the members of scheduled castes and scheduled tribes communities. Statutory land reforms became agenda to show development of SCs and STs.

In Madhya Pradesh also reducing the Charnoi land from 7.5 per cent to 2 per cent, gave a possibility to redistribute land to landless SCs and STs. But the major concern about the quality of land and feasibly to reap benefits remained unattended. Ambedkar opined that evil of small holdings was not only fundamental but it was derived from maladjustment in our social economy.

He advocated state socialism essential for fostering economic development with justice. Under the state socialism agriculture would be the state industry and farms should be cultivated as collective farms. Sen (1962) also supported that family-based peasants farm were found to be more productive. It was also evident that medium holdings (5–10 acres) were far more productive than large holdings (Nanchariah, 1995).

The distribution of Charnoi land to scheduled castes and scheduled tribes of Madhya Pradesh was done following the Bhopal Document and the demand of the Dalits for land. But, unfortunately the philosophy of Ambedkar with regard to land reforms was totally ignored. There was a golden opportunity in the form of land redistribution diverted from Charnoi land in Madhya Pradesh where philosophy of Ambedkar could have been implemented very successfully for sustainable development of scheduled castes and scheduled tribes in the form of collective farming.

Instead of distributing land of small size, attempts should have been made to encourage collective farming. That could have been possible among the kith and kin of a scheduled caste or scheduled tribe family to ensure sustainability of benefits received from the state favour. However, since the landless have been made marginal and small landowners, that may not help them much as there are doubts with regard to productive and accumulation of problems currently being faced by the marginal and small farmers.

Thus, it is very much evident that in the ambiguity of meaning of land reforms and ignoring the caste as the important dimension in land ownership, it has become more a political agenda just to distribute the land among landless labourers. Land is more a social status in villages, particularly to large land owning communities who are mostly non-scheduled groups than a productive asset for scheduled groups mainly because the agriculture in the country is largely dependent upon mansoon and no serious attempts have been made to ensure irrigation facilities to new landowners and to the marginal and small farmers as most of them belonging to SCs and STs.

The unsustainability in the land reforms also lies in the fact that these reforms were not integrated attempts to ensure the benefits to the new landowners who were mainly poor landless labourers and had no means to accumulate means of production sufficient enough to sustain their economy and thus fell into debt trap after becoming land owners.

The crop pattern in Madhya Pradesh shows that the production and productivity of Jowar, a sustainable crop of the region from socio-economic and ecological perspectives, had decreased sharply particularly after the new economic reforms. But the crop pattern changed towards cash crops like soyabean and cotton that were sown in large landholdings and were more profitable to non-scheduled groups mainly because of having facilities of mechanical harvesting and transport to the markets. The production was high mainly due to intensive modern agricultural techniques, which were not at all available to small and marginal farmers, a majority of whom belong to SCs and STs.

Agricultural science and technology in our country has led to great revolutions but no innovations were made in the indigenous and traditional techniques of marginal and small farmers. This is also a clear case of caste and class discrimination. The large-scale migration of small and marginal landowning communities is mainly due to such skewed development. Therefore, studies would be required to ascertain whether cash crops might further marginalize weaker sections.

Thus, the unsustainability lies in the mismatched context of practical planning of technical know-how which often get support of and implemented for the cost-bearing class and large asset owning communities. Scheduled castes and scheduled tribes lack in both these aspects, hence, remain deprived and discriminated. The sustainable development of scheduled castes and scheduled tribes can only be ensured if the land reforms are integrated with the innovations and upgradation of indigenous technologies so that production from the given land exceeds the wages earned by them from labour.

It is further emphasized that, caste-based discrimination and segmentation in factor markets in organized private sector were incompatible with the objective of growth and distribution which were pursued under large-scale privatization as part of the New Economic Reforms (Thorat, 1998). The biggest question is how to annihilate the caste barrier? One thing is certain that in the Indian society, the caste dynamics are changing and it is the proper time to change the wind in favour of scheduled castes and scheduled tribes and in that sense in the favour of all the castes and sections that have remained marginalized, deprived and exploited.

That question relates to attitude of people also. For social justice and development, ecoethical concerns should become the priority concerns (Verma, 1994, 1995). The major question in sustainable development also rests upon values and attitude of people towards socio-economic and ecological order (Verma, 1999). The existing distribution of resources and income was a continued function of the past undemocratic system of deprivation to lower and privileges to higher in the social order, which simply perpetuate inequality and injustices in the society (Verma and Sohrot, 2003). In fact, roles of individuals or groups in our country are still mainly guided by their social status. Elites among SCs and STs of Madhya Pradesh are playing their roles efficiently and effectively but once they come out of the power gambit, they become totally helpless.

The paper, thus, brings out and establishes the fact that the caste dynamics have been largely ignored in planning for the economic development of SCs and STs in Madhya Pradesh. For sustainable development of SCs and STs, due recognition to the existing social dynamics of caste in the policy and programmes meant for their economic development is essential.

References

Agrawal, Bina, (2001), Economics and Other Social Sciences: An Inevitable Debate? *Contributions to Indian Sociology*, Vol. 35, No. 5, p. 389.

Ambedkar, B.R., (1918), Small Holdings in India and their Remedies, *Journal of Indian Economic Society*. Reproduced in the *Dr Babasaheb Ambedkar Writings and Speeches,* (ed.), Vasant Moon, Vol. I, Government of Maharashtra.

Ambedkar, B.R., (1979), *Dr Babasaheb Ambedkar Writings and Speeches*., (ed.), Vasant Moon, Voila, p. 455, Government of Maharashtra.

Ambedkar, B.R., (1987), The Hindu Social Order: Its Essential Features, in *Dr Babasaheb Ambedkar Writings and Speeches*, (ed.), Vasant Moon, Vol. 3, Department of Education, Government of Maharashtra.

Ambedkar, Nagendra, (1992), Evaluation Study of Integrated Rural Development Programme in Jabera Block, Damoh District, MP, *Research Abstracts*, Publication No. 6, BANISS, p. 24.

Appu, P.S., (1996), *Land Reforms in India: A Survey of Policy and Legislation and Implementation*, Vikas Publishing House Pvt. Ltd., New Delhi.

Deshpande, R.S. and Sukhdeo Thorat, (2000), Caste and Economic Inequality: Unexplained Evidence with Respect to the Dalits, *AJSDJ*, Vol. VIII, 1–35.

Dreze, Jean and Amartya Sen, (1999), *India: Economic Development and Social Opportunity,* Oxford University Press, New Delhi, 9th Edn.

Gadkar, R.D., (1998), Human Resource Development, Utilization and Change among the Scavenger with special reference to Indore (MP), *Research Abstracts*, Publication No. 6, BANISS, p. 63.

Gadkar, R.D. and R.D. Maurya, (1998), Social-economic Factors for Disabilities and Causes of Commissioning of Atrocities by non-SCs and STs, *Research Abstracts*, Publication No. 6, BANISS, p. 5.

Government of India: Sixth Five-Year Plan, 1978–83, Chapter 13.

Joshi, Y.G., (1992), Group Mobilization and Transfer of Dryland Farming Technology for Water Conservation and Income Enhancement of the Farmers of Malwa Region, MP, *Research Abstracts*, Publication No. 6, BANISS, p. 79.

Joshi, Y.G., (1992), Evaluation of the New Tendu Patta Policy of MP: An Appraisal, *Research Abstracts,* Publication No. 6, BANISS, p. 24.

Joshi, Y.G., (1994), Tribal Migration and Man-Power Planning in Jhabua (MP), *Research Abstracts*, Publication No. 6, BANISS, p. 72.

Joshi, Y.G., (1994), Evaluation Study of the Scheme of Post-matric Scholarship to the Scheduled Castes and Scheduled Tribes in Madhya Pradesh and Rajasthan, *Research Abstracts*, Publication No. 6, BANISS, p. 27.

Joshi, Y.G., (1998), Perception of Drought and the Adoption of Control Strategy in the Jhabua, MP, *Research Abstracts,* Publication No. 6, BANISS, p. 83.

Joshi, Y.G. and D.K. Verma, (1999), Aspirations and Achievements of Scheduled Castes in the Last Five Decades of Independent India: A Pilot Study in Madhya Pradesh, *Research Abstracts*, Publication No. 6, BANISS, p. 48.

Joshi, Y.G. and D.K. Verma, (1999), Census Data based Study on the Baiga Scheduled Tribe of MP, *Research Abstracts*, Publication No. 6, BANISS, p. 85.

Joshi, Y.G. and D.K. Verma, (2000), Seasonal Rural Out-migration from Chhattisgarh Region with special reference to the Scheduled Castes and Scheduled Tribes Communities, *Research Abstracts*, Publication No. 6, BANISS, p. 75.

Joshi, Y.G. and D.K. Verma, (2000), Register of Handicraft Artisans of MP, *Research Abstracts*, Publication No. 6, BANISS, p. 105.

Killick, Tony, (1989), A Reaction Too Far: Economic Theory and the Role of the State in Developing Countries, Overseas Development Institute, London.

Maurya, R.D., (1996), Tribals and Panchayati Raj in Madhya Pradesh, *Research Abstracts,* Publication No. 6, BANISS, p. 81.

Maurya, R.D., (1998), Impact of Special Component Plan on Socio-Economic Development of Scheduled Castes in Madhya Pradesh with special reference to Rural Development and Forestry Sector, *Research Abstracts*, Publication No. 6, BANISS, p. 38.

Maurya, R.D., (2001), Impact of Special Component Plan on Socio-economic Development of Scheduled Castes in Madhya Pradesh, *Journal of Rural Development*, Vol. 20 (I), pp. 131–151.

Maurya, R.D., (2002), A Comparative Study of the Scheduled Castes Financial Development Corporation Programmes for the Socio-economic Upliftment of the Scheduled Castes in AP and MP, *Research Abstracts*, Publication No. 6, BANISS, p. 56.

Nagar, V.D. and K.P. Nagar, (1992), *Economic Thoughts and Policy of Dr Ambedkar,* Segment Books, New Delhi, pp. 115–120.

Naik, C.D., (1999), Degree of Untouchability in the Rural India with special reference to Mhow Tehsil, *Research Abstracts*, Publication No. 6, BANISS, p. 9.

Nanachariah, G., (1995), Dr Ambedkar on Small Holdings and Reorganization of Structure of Agriculture in India, AJSDJ, Vol. III, pp. 1–19.

Nanachariah, G., (1997), Dr Ambedkar of Fiscal and Monetary System in Colonial India: The Relevance, *AJSDJ*, Vol. V, pp. 26–37.

Ram Nandu, (1987), *The Mobile Scheduled Castes: Rise of a New Middle Class,* Delhi, Hindustan Publishing Corporation.

Ram Nandu, (2002), Abstraction to Substantiation: Ambedkar's Thoughts on Justice and Social Equality in Contemporary Perspective and Development, *AJSDJ*, Vol. X, pp. 1–20.

Renuka, V., (1999), Human Development Report for Madhya Pradesh: Some Hidden Truths, *EPW*.

Sen, A.K., (1992), *Inequality Re-examined*, Oxford University Press, New Delhi.

Sen, A., (1999), *Development as Freedom*, Oxford University Press, New Delhi.

Sharma, K., (1998), Bedia Women: Survey and Rehabilitation Strategies, *Research Abstracts*, Publication No. 6, BANISS, p. 97.

Sharma, K., (2001), The Socio-economic and Political Status of Women of the Scheduled Castes and Scheduled Tribes of MP, *Research Abstracts*, Publication No. 6, BANISS, p. 99.

Sharma, K., (2001), Girl Infanticide in Chambal Division: A Report, *Research Abstracts*, Publication No. 6, BANISS, p. 102.

Singh, R.G., (1997), Nature, Extent, Causes and Control of Atrocities on the Scheduled Castes in MP *Research Abstracts*, Publication No. 6, BANISS, pl.

Singh, R.G., (2000), Status of Scavenging and Scavengers in MP, *Research Abstracts*, Publication No. 6, BANISS, p. 67.

Singh, R.G., (2002), Atrocity on Scheduled Castes: A Case Study of Village Kolukhedi, District Bhopal, p. 18.

Subramanian, S., (2000), *India's Economic Performance and Reforms: A Perspective for the New Millennium*, Konark Publishers Private Limited, New Delhi.

Thorat, S.K., (1997), Economic Progress of Scheduled Castes under Five Year Plans, *AJSDJ*, Vol. V, pp. 45–55.

Thorat, S.K., (1998), New Economic Policy and Its Impact on Employment and Poverty of the Scheduled Castes: Some Observations, *AJSDJ*, Vol. VI, pp. 15–32.

Verma, D.K., (1993), Inter-generational Equity: Environmental Right of the Child, *AJSDJ*, Vol. III, pp. 163–168.

Verma, D.K., (1994), Eco-ethical Approach for Sustainable Development and Social Justice. *AJSDJ*:2, pp. 37–59.

Verma, D.K., (1995), Ecological Sustainability in Social Development, in *Social Development and Justice*, Radiant Publishers, New Delhi, pp. 225–229.

Verma, D.K., (1997), Dr B.R. Ambedkar's Views on Planning, Development and Conservation of Environmental Resources, *AJSDJ*:5, pp. 1–8.

Verma, D.K., (1997), Social Forestry and Weaker Sections: Effectiveness of Social Forestry Programme in Environmental Conservation and Increasing Resource Availability with particular reference to Weaker Sections, *Research Abstracts*, Publication No. 6, BANISS, p. 34.

Verma, D.K., (1998), Role of Social Forestry Programme in the Development of Scheduled Castes and Scheduled Tribes, *AJSDJ*, Vol. VI, pp. 53–69.

Verma, D.K., (1999), A Study of Centrally Sponsored Scheme of Post-matric Scholarship to Students belonging to the Scheduled Castes and Scheduled Tribes in MP, *Research Abstracts*, Publication No. 6, BANISS, p. 42.

Verma, D.K., (1999), Sustainable Development, Madhya Pradesh, *Journal of Social Sciences*, Vol. 4, No. 2, pp. 37–59.

Verma, D.K., (1999b), Concept and Dimensions of Social Environment Needed for Sustainable Development, in *Social Environment for Sustainable Development*, published by Rawat Publications, Jaipur.

Verma, D.K., (2000b), Dr Ambedkar's Economic Philosophy and Implications of New Economic reforms on Employment of Scheduled Castes, p. 104, in *Impact of Economic Reforms on SCs and STs* edited by K.P. Kumaran, NIRD, Hyderabad.

Verma, D.K. and A. Sohrot, (2003), The Concept of Social Justice in Post-modern Society: Some Reflections on Sustainable Development, *Prashasnika*, Vol. XXX, No. 2, pp. 39–59.

Verma, D.K. and Sohrot, (2002), Research Abstracts (Summaries and Recommendations of Research Projects, 1992–2002). Institute's Publications, No. 6, Dr Babasaheb Ambedkar National Institute of Social Sciences, Mhow.

Verma, D.K. and Y.G. Joshi, (2000), Social Segregation, Accessibility to Amenities and Level of Integration of Scheduled Castes Basties in Villages of MP, *Research Abstracts*, Publication No. 6, BANISS, p. 12.

World Bank, (1999), World Development Report 2000-02: *Attacking Poverty*, Oxford University Press, p. 34.

3

Dalit Liberation, Liberalization and Liberalism

NIRAJ KUMAR JHA

The Government of India embarked on the path of liberalization in 1991. Though piecemeal and lackadaisical reforms have started showing results. The current growth rate of 8 per cent is one of the highest in the world. Foreign exchange reserves are spilling and foreign investments are pouring in. More and more Indians are joining the international club of billionaires and salaries in various sectors have skyrocketed.[1] At the same time, there is a rapid growth of Indian multinationals. Markets are full of commodities and shoppers and the shortages of the past are only fast vanishing bad memories of the middle-aged. The apprehension towards globalization in the Indian corporate sector is a matter of past and they are making global strides. At the other end, there is substantial reduction in poverty levels.[2] However, responses to the process have been mixed depending on the ideology or interest of the respondent. Dalits view the launch of economic reforms in 1991 and their subsequent expansion with scepticism.[3] They are exception as an identity group in this respect; nonetheless, they do not regard themselves purely as an identity group.

Who/What is Dalit?

The term 'Dalit' is an identity marker of ex-untouchables communities consisting nearly 16 per cent of India's population, who are described as the scheduled castes (SCs) in the governmental parlance. From ancient times they have been suffering a totally dehumanized existence. Still they struggle to get basic dignity and rights. In independent India, driven by democracy and self-consciousness, they seek to redeem their humanity. In this endeavour, they discarded the names given by others which were or were found to be either degrading or patronizing and adopted the term 'Dalit' as an identity marker. The transformation of the stigmatized identity of these erstwhile untouchables to a self-chosen identity as Dalit is a story of collective struggle waged over centuries. Dalit is a political identity, as opposed to a caste one. It expresses Dalits' knowledge of themselves as oppressed people and signifies their resolve to demand liberation through a revolutionary transformation of the system that oppresses them.[4] In this sense Dalit denotes a 'substantialization'[5] process across categories of untouchable outcastes on a pan-Indian basis. It behaves like a class, as a social category having so perceived common economic interests to be defended or to be pursued; like a political group having its own rights to gain and defend and an ideology of liberation and advancement. Dalit, thus, denotes three things, viz., cultural identity, economic interest and political ideology.

Dalits and Liberalization

An ideological perspective seeks to comprehend the milieu which it seeks to change. For the Dalit ideology the reforms of 1991 unsettled the ground realities. The government which was the focus and target of their revolutionary strategy suddenly started to withdraw it on the commanding heights and ground was thrown open to private and foreign players. Command economy gradually allowed the market to operate according to its own rules to an extent. Market economy was an area in which Dalits hardly have any foothold and where they have (the government) began eroding. "The fact remains, however, that all CEOs and billionaires happen to be non-Dalits and members of all industry organizations are non-Dalits. The exclusion of Dalits from trade and industry is real. There is no Dalit, bourgeoisie or Dalits don't form part of the Indian bourgeoisie."[6] In such a situation, they suspect that the roll-back of the government would undo everything that they have achieved through the reservation route and preferential welfare measures. The subsequent expansion of reforms deepened their worries. With the global trends of liberalization, privatization and globalization (LPG) of which India has become an active participant (and the presumed retreat of the government in that wake), they find that the single avenue of social mobility available to them has now been blocked.[7]

The fears are not unfounded. The social justice measures were patronizing and their coverage was never comprehensive. The vast majority of Dalits remained untouched by these measures. A middle class did emerge out of the Dalits but their achievements remained dependent on the government support. The concern caused by the prospect of the state backtracking among such people is genuine. Nevertheless, the conceptualization of the problem is not always well-founded.

Genesis of Reforms

The launch of reforms in India was more a response to a crisis rather than a well-planned move. The command economy model of India by the close of 1980s had completely exhausted whatever potential it had despite some reformist tinkering by the Rajiv Gandhi government. The crisis surfaced in the form of the dramatic depleting of foreign exchange reserves which at one time fell to a level which was not enough to cover more than two weeks of imports (July 1991). It was this crisis which pushed India for initiating economic reforms.[8]

The quasi-socialist economic model was no longer sustainable and reforms were the only recourse available. India was not alone in this predicament; the crisis had engulfed the entire socialist bloc and revolutions and reforms were the order of the day. Later, India as a participant of GATT negotiations became a member of the WTO, in which all member states enter economic relations on uniform terms. The new global regime has made reforms obligatory. Choices are obvious: remain part of the comity of nations or become an international pariah and if the choice is to remain part of the international economic order which is highly competitive then the choice is—perform or perish.

Reforms, in fact, have no alternative. At the least, it is something like a *Manuvadi* ploy. On the contrary, it is the rejection of a system which supported the Brahminical ethos. The ideology which India had adopted earlier was an adaptation of the western evolutionary socialism combined with the Soviet socialist craft. The ideology suited the psyche of the then Indian leadership largely constituted by Brahmins, as it was similar in ethos to the Brahmanism which latently supported a class of abysmally uncreative and non-productive people to lord over the society. The system privileged and glorified the class which virtually contributed nothing and was totally, parasitic in existence. The imperial order too, to an extent was similar in nature. The Indian society was subjugated to the requirements of the imperial nation and in order to fulfil that objective, the colonized people were directly enslaved to the people manning the imperial order here in India. After independence, the brown sahibs who inherited the 'burden' of their erstwhile white masters found socialism most suited to their status and taste. They became the benefactors of uneducated, impoverished and backward people. Their ideology was the new avatar of earlier civilizing mission which was the worst statement of the imperial duplicity; the civilizing mission was latently the heinous ploy and justification for debasing a whole civilization, enslaving their existence and appropriating their resources. In independent India, the ideology in mutation benefited only a handful of people, viz., bureaucrats, professional politicians and trade union leaders and functioned detrimentally towards the general interests, particularly its economy and the people.

Liberalization and Liberalism

Reforms are unavoidable but it does not mean that they are undesirable or evil. In fact reforms, which seek to liberalize economy, are the crying need of the hour not only for the sake of development but also for the sake of human dignity and democracy. Liberalization is premised on the recognition of the worth of a single individual. It bestows faith in the ability and the intentions of individual human beings. Liberalism is respect for individuality. It restricts but only for the sake of coexistence or in order to thwart the designs of evil intent. But ideally, restrictive tendencies are to be minimalist. The government is basically the enforcer of contracts and obligations, written or by convention. In this sense, liberalism is not an imposed system but an evolved system. It is a state in which free individuals self-manage their co-existence.

The essential credo of liberalism in this sense is democracy, that is to say, people manage their affairs by their own. It is not problematic where liberalism is by-product of social change. But where liberalism is being adopted in a pre-modern setup, problems are inevitable. In such societies there are gross inequalities. There are hierarchies and also there is a hierarchy of hierarchies, which hinder the equal participation in public decision-making or even mere participation of those people who are located at lower rungs of social hierarchy. If liberalization effort is genuine and its institutionalization is proper, it is bound to attain its natural state resulting in gradual withering away of multiplicity of hierarchies and the economic hierarchy would not entail gross deprivation or degradation of the people of the low status.

Liberalism reflects the very nature of human beings. Human beings are above all economic beings. They manipulate nature and create a continuous chain of production, distribution, exchange and consumption. However, humans are also not passive workers. Their natural tendency is to innovate and improve their lot. Human beings are basically enterprising. Liberalism seeks to liberate this tendency from accentuated sway of another human tendency, i.e., to dominate. When human's natural and associative urges are unrestrained and disruptive tendencies are at check, there is a flowering of good senses—empathy as well sympathy. Unfortunate people who fall behind are cared. Companies make non-profit investments for the betterment of general life. However, such practices are not charities that makes strong economic sense. In the contemporary context such acts of public good are the most effective publicity campaign as the goodwill and reputation so gained is economically very rewarding for the contributing companies. On macro-level, reduced poverty means better business opportunities for the corporate sector. The concept in the corporate world is termed as corporate social responsibility (CSR). Traditionally viewed as drain on profits, now this is being regarded as an investment with multiple payoffs for the corporation.[9]

Thus freedom is the essential ingredient of liberalism. All individuals are free to participate in the public affairs on equal footing and to avail the equality of opportunities. Further, the free association of free individuals in order to remain so have inbuilt mechanism for saving its members from destitution and deprivation and adequate protection for people who are challenged otherwise—physically, mentally or by age. The system is thus the product of freedom and the system in turn enables people to remain free. The free people are capable of utilizing their faculties and abilities to the optimum. This leads to general material prosperity, cultural efflorescence and refinement of moral values.

When entrepreneurship becomes a general culture, individuals are not seen in primordial light but they are seen from economic perspective and any person who eats and works is not worthless in a freely operating market. There are aspects of liberalism which negate primordial identities and parochial values:

1. Liberalism recognizes individual, not ethnic groupings, as units of society.
2. Liberalism in practice stands for unrestrained enterprise.
3. A general culture of free enterprise takes cognizance of human beings as economic beings.

Ideally liberalism is thus antithetical to ethnic identities and it has innate mechanism for ensuring that no life suffers inhuman degradation. This is reflected by the high level institutionalization of social security in the developed liberal democracies. In the case of India, a fully developed liberal system would undermine caste and caste-based discriminations in particular and would ensure against destitution. This resolves the basic problems of Dalits, who are socially challenged. The society not only denies them dignity and equal opportunity but also resist their efforts to come out of their degraded existence.

India's Illiberal Order Hindered Social Justice

The opposite of the liberal order is the collectivized order in which individuality of people is denied. They became part of a collective whole in which their roles are largely predetermined. And they work and consume on provisions. And, in such a system there emerges a managerial class which becomes all powerful. With managers assuming the mantle of masters, individuals become dependent clients losing both their identity (individuality) and freedom. And like feudalism of yore, such systems become stagnant soon after their constitution and decay sets in as soon as they lose dynamism. Such systems guarantee neither equality, which they espouse so vehemently, nor freedom and in the end there is left nothing but destitution. Moreover, people prohibited from pursuing their natural selves and consolidating their abilities and efforts materially turn to identity politics and indulge in all sorts of negativism including religious bigotry. A system is dynamic only when its each and every constituent is free to develop his/her potential to the fullest and to contribute to the best of his/her capacity. Collectivized orders of the twentieth centuries were either destroyed by their own evil designs or collapsed under their own dead weights. Few survive but not without liberalizing their economies.

There have been several variants of the collectivized orders. India was one with its quasi-socialist economy. While the worst of the collectivized orders, i.e., Fascism or Nazism allowed neither political, nor economic and nor even personal freedom, the socialist orders while restricted political and economic freedoms but left some space for personal freedom, the Indian model denied only economic freedom. But among all these three freedoms, this freedom is crucial one. In the absence of this freedom the economy hardly moved, whatever growth was possible was due to the infusion of new technologies and the growth of population. The state ran crucial industries by its own and controlled the rest. For the personnel of the state, the government's mastery on economy was extremely profitable enterprise without any personal investment or risk. For the rest business became a cumbersome drudgery with little incentive to grow.[10] Only those profited and became rich outside the organizational fold of the government, who could bribe, cajole and manipulate the personnel of the government.

The regime, which India is gradually dismantling, not only hindered growth but also negated justice and equity to a large extent. In such an environment any sort of social change was only a chimera. The general servitude caused not only material poverty but also moral and cultural poverty. As a result, the massive majority of depressed classes remained exploited, humiliated and poverty-stricken. Yet the dominant notion is that the earlier regime espoused social justice and supported Dalits. It also generated the impression that the social justice measures implemented by the welfare socialist state were inadequate but correct and they were being abandoned for the benefit of international capitalism under the neo-imperial pressures. Indeed, through reservations and other welfare measures the government facilitated social mobility of a number of Dalits. But overall, this gives a very misleading picture. All those numbers constituted only a minuscule minority of the Dalit communities. The prevalent large-scale deprivation of the huge majority of subaltern among Dalits and the continued denial of dignity to them negates the efficacy of those measures. However, the impression it created, was the success of the intrinsic nature of the model, it was a showcase model of social development in which a limited number of the people were provided with the opportunity to move ahead mainly for the purpose of showcasing. Not to speak of the Dalits alone, the vast majority of society remained oppressed and deprived.

Moreover, the social justice scheme was not aimed at the democratic reorganization of the society. That was more a strategy of creating elites out of these communities and placating those sections with the purpose of co-opting these marginalized people with this symbolic assimilation into the new dispensation. This was a part of the larger design of legitimization of the power structure. Even the British imperialists did the same by offering some crumbs of the imperial pie to the native elites. On the eve of the independence, the opportunism of the people in the helms of affairs put the real democratization on the backburner but for the legitimization sake the new regime required such measures.

The modernization project which started with the colonial rule and the developmental project of the Government of India since independence did help in lessening the caste-based segregations and dehumanizing taboos in social relations. In workforces of large factories, in educational institutions and to a large extent in upper echelons of bureaucracy and government, caste-identity became irrelevant as the determinant of social status. The founding fathers had a broader vision of democracy as social democracy[11] and systemic inclusion of such social democratic goals led to improvement in the conditions of depressed peoples including that of Dalits, however the overall scenario remained dismal and whatever changes occurred were superficial, segmented and confined to pockets. Moreover the selective approach of social justice was not only beset with limited potential but was also not viable or sustainable. This is testified by huge backlogs of reserved seats meant for the scheduled castes and scheduled tribes, year after year and now diminished entry of Dalits in government services. It is estimated that for every ten Dalits retiring from government jobs, less than two are getting in.[12] This proves the point that the reservation policy has not empowered the Dalits but only made them dependent.

Their rise is unsustainable without government support. The social engineering is very shallow in this case.

The basic problem was that such closed and controlled economy with its inherent culture of corruption had very limited scope of expansion and so was its ability to ensure social mobility. Amidst this constraint, the democratic regime had the mandate to deliver, i.e., to ensure social equity. The government in this direction adopted a model which resembles sanskritization[13], which allowed limited mobility for the deprived sections of society in the traditional set-up. Through reservations and other welfare measures the government made space for a selective few to move out of squalor. This symbolic mobility was workable; this showcased the ability and intentions of the people in the helms of affairs and created a false hope for the deprived people. And, for the limited success of the measures, such phantoms like neo-imperialism and capitalism were blamed. The fate of the massive majority however remained unchanged. The feudal economic and political order remained unscathed and so the old mindsets (of patron and client relationships). Fundamentally there was no change. Change did not have even the scope of sanskritization, which ensured, if successful, mobility for a whole community of a particular locality. The government sponsored sanskritization, only snatched some families and some individuals out of some family into the fold of the power structure.

Dalit Liberation

The closed and controlled economy also resulted in closed minds of the people in which parochial identities and primordial values ruled the roots. Liberalization aims at ensuring the economic freedom of people and unleashing their entrepreneurial potential, which in the case of Indians is legendary. A scratch on the surface, what actually the economic reforms so far have been, made the Indian economy one of the fastest growing in the world. One can imagine the velocity of the explosion of the productive potentials of Indians if a proper churning is made. The massive production of wealth would wipe out poverty from this huge landmass forever. Elimination of poverty itself would be one of the biggest factors for the end of caste-based discriminations. Poverty and caste position were interlinked. Noted sociologist M.N. Srinivas writes, “Another pan-Indian phenomenon was the existence of a larger overlap between landlessness and traditional ‘untouchable’ castes, a fact which enhanced their poverty, misery, and exploitability.”[14] In fact, whatever jolt the ascribed status of Dalits received was in the new market relations, in the ambience of large industries and in the new cosmopolitan cities where caste-based discriminations were not so pronounced and debilitating. However, the socialistic agenda of the government did not let the modernization project to really take off the agenda hindered both, growth and egalitarianism-economic as well as cultural. Now, liberalization along with globalization aims at loosening the grip of bureaucracy and politicians on economy. This is expected to unleash the huge entrepreneurial potentials of Indians leading to high growth, which is being witnessed today. India is one of the fastest growing economies in the world and the level of poverty is going down simultaneously. It would benefit one and all. And higher social mobility horizontally and vertically would also weaken caste identity and open the minds of the people

Further, the onset of the knowledge economy and globalization of economy would leave little space for caste-based discriminatory practices. Such ways are symptomatic of the traditional or pre-modern economic order based on agriculture, household handicraft and jajmani-based services. While modernity with its industry and impersonal market relations weakened the order of caste-based discriminations, the post-modern economy has the full potential of wiping out this social anomaly. New economy along with the expansion of traditional industries would gradually diminish the role of agriculture in the economy. Modernized (and corporatised) agriculture would be less dependent on numbers than on technology and capital. And people, particularly the marginal farmers for whom agriculture is highly unsustainable profession and landless labourers, would move out of villages. M.N. Srinivas notes the trend, “A new feature of village life is the emigration of large numbers of people both seasonally and on a long-term basis. Prosperous agricultural areas are attracting labourers from poorer areas ... . Fast growing cities also attract migrants form rural areas. ... Rapid population growth and the breakdown of the jajmani system are some of the ‘push’ factors for emigration.”[15] With less proportion of people indulging in agriculture and even lesser number of people living in villages would make traditional social relations based on caste domination, patron-client relationships and pollution and purity passe. Even otherwise urbanization, opening of the village economy and availability of alternative means of employment have lessened the dependence of Dalits on the jajmani type economic relations and enabled them to assert their dignity.[16] Similarly, the nationwide movement of labour and their cash" remittances have made their families in villages to greater freedom from degradation as a result of lesser dependence on the dominant castes.[17] In fact, the traditional settings themselves are cesspools germinating the vices of caste domination and exploitation. The problem, for instance, has been identified in an editorial of a leading newspaper "...Despite legislation like the Scheduled Castes and Scheduled Tribes (Prevention of Atrocities) Act, 1989, the state has failed to crack down on caste violence. Steps to make grass-roots politics more representative have also been met with resistance from the upper castes. What is worrying is even states like Tamil Nadu, which have made remarkable progress in human development indicators, including literacy, have failed to resolve the caste divide ... . Most of rural India is yet to accept the idea of an inclusive India. Economic and political empowerment of Dalits continues to be resisted by non-Dalit castes across the country. Resistance by oppressed communities is met with violence, often with the tacit support of state officials. In Tamil Nadu, caste Hindus have refused to accept Dalit presidents in many panchayats reserved for the community. Elected Dalit panchayat presidents in Madurai and Vuudunagar districts have been pressurized to resign by non-Dalits, defeating the idea of Panchayati Raj institutions becoming agents of economic development and social justice." The identification of problem is appropriate but resolutions smacks of bureaucratism, "These incidents reflect the failure of public institutions and political parties to make the polity democratic and egalitarian. Strict enforcement of laws by the state can address these problems to a large extent. The process of social transformation will have to be coercive if the non-Dalits, including those from the backward castes, refuse to share power by consensus".[18] The editor ignores the fact that such acts are perpetrated only with the connivance of the law enforcement agencies, instances of which are cited in the same editorial. In fact, there is no need to involve police as far as social transformation is concerned. Their performance even in their most elemental tasks is horrendously lacking. In fact, there is no need of such type of social engineering. Modernization and now postmodernism (the knowledge economy) in their logical course would lead to massive urbanization; only a tiny proportion of population would live in the villages. In that case, the Dalit problem would be over (substantially) automatically.

In modern and post-modern megapolicies, caste is the last thing which comes between individuals interacting. Even in the realms of personal and cultural, like matrimony and other social relations (not economic), caste is playing diminishing role. Planning of bigger but ecology and people-friendly cities or city-states (self-governing mega-cities), which invite people rather than repel, would be the biggest feat in social engineering. At the same time, the expansion of the middle class in India as a result of the economic growth of the country is driving caste out of their social relations.[19]

Misconceptions about Liberalization

It is also an unfounded belief that there would be lesser number of government jobs available under the liberalization regime. It would only lead to the rationalization of jobs. The feudalistic state apparatus would be more business like. The unnecessary and unproductive jobs would be cut and resultant restructuring dividends would enable the government to hire more personnel to staff its regulatory, facilitating and arbitration jobs. It would also make the government enlarge the representation of the people. Further, efficient and cost-effective governance would result in larger surplus for the entrepreneurial class which is the gunpowder for developmental explosion. Once society is prosperous, the government would also be in a position to hire larger number of people. In fact, our governance is in need of more personnel rather badly. We need more judges, more police personnel, more doctors and more teachers, to cite only a few types of services where personnel population ratios are too low.

At the same time, if government frees itself from doing business which is not its business, it would be better equipped to focus on its essential tasks, viz., criminal justice, maintenance of law and order, regulation and facilitation of economic affairs, maintenance of public utilities, education, health and disaster management, etc. Additionally, it could also be a very effective instrument of social engineering if it sheds its flab. This realization has downed upon now even on the political class across the spectrum of ideologies. At the India Today Conclave 2006, Arun Jaitley from the BJP said, "Market helps state and state helps poor." On the other hand, Sitaram Yechury of the CPM Politburo exhorted, "Bring poor into the market". Yechury cited the Peruvian economist, Hernando De Soto in his speech and Soto addressed later the same conclave via satellite and said quoting studies and surveys from across the world and his own experiences in Peru that markets can serve the masses if people have legal attributes like property entitlements or other documentary proofs of their value or the value of their business.[20]

The liberation of Dalits rests on the success of the liberalization. The vast economic opportunities thrown open by LPG combined with the power of India in knowledge economy would create large number of jobs. Simultaneous growth of services and industries fuelled by India's rise in knowledge economy would require larger workforce. Unburdened agriculture would also be more productive. All these things are happening; only their speed is checked by old mindsets. In the workforce of the new economy, caste would be of no relevance. The Dalits must focus on how to make best of the new opportunity rather than to resist it. It is also a misconception that liberalization works against social equity. Instead liberalization needs equity in order to succeed. The World Bank's 2006 World Development Report argues the same. 'Greater equity fosters greater prosperity'. In an article, suitably titled, "All that you can't leave behind; growth bandwagon cannot afford to exclude the poor", Frangois Bourguignon and Shantayanan Devarajan, Chief Economist, World Bank, and Bank's Chief Economist, South Asian Region respectively, argue that the lack of opportunities harms initiative and deprives societies of the talent and efforts of some of its members. Societies that start off with an inequitable distribution of resources tend to put in place inequitable economic and political institutions. So, inequity is perpetuated across generations, because elites control power and capture the benefits from economic activities. This is not only unjust; it is economically inefficient. Elites that capture power to their own benefit prevent large parts of the population from realizing their economic potential.[21] Liberalization in order to succeed, in which now even domestic capitalists have developed a stake, requires the empowerment of the hitherto marginalized people.

Further, if the corporate sector comes under laissez faire with adequate safeguards for concerns like environmental protection and public safety, they would be under moral pressure to fulfil their social responsibility. If not, they can be persuaded to do the same. In fact, during the socialist regime their all energies were concentrated on getting away from the governmental, strangle hold. They were constrained not to think morally. Now, the corporate sector has started to respond to their social responsibilities. They would also be ready for affirmative action once they consolidate their position in the globally integrated economy in which they were thrown in all of a sudden after decades of complacency. They have come out of the shell only 14 years ago, says Gurcharan Das, corporate man, writer and columnist, "Give us another 10 years and we can show the world what we can do". Only caution he pleads, "Anything the government does is the kiss of death. It should allow business to grow by distancing itself and removing barriers to such growth."[22]

Dalits can throw away their bondages denying their dignity and freedom not through traditional means like religious reforms and legally enforced social behaviour but by modern and post-modern means. Traditional orders should rather be rejected than reformed.[23] Modernism through its system of mass-production and cosmopolitanism of modern cities dealt a severe blow to caste-based segregations. Now, new technological revolution based on information technology and increased mobility of people within and beyond state boundaries (as a result of LPG) are making such categories growingly out of date and abandoned. In fact, liberalization with post-modern economic conditions offers fresh opportunities for the Dalits in their struggle for dignity and better living conditions.

Pitfalls in the Way of Liberalization

However, old prejudices may linger in several segments of society and that can be eradicated by democratization of general ethos and mass culture. The Dalits are the most active agents of democratization today. People should align with them in order to strengthen democracy and they should also align with other democratic movements. Movements for gender justice, environmental protection and human rights and like others are interlinked. In this context, the most powerful democratic development is liberalization itself. Dalits have greater stake in the process than others. They should aid the process for liberalization rather than jeopardize this. The process promises to give powers in the hands of people. At the same time, Dalits must resist ghettoised and divisive world views of solidarity. Self-respect is the key to the cause of Dalit advancements (Periyar propagated and proved this fact).[24] Self-respect automatically translates into respect for fellow human beings.

The Dalits continue to be at the receiving end of the socio-political set-up, as Gohana incident recently suggests. But the political mobilization in that wake and the countrywide networking they demonstrated are very encouraging.[25] More pronounced and perhaps more effective is the rise of an activist scholarship among Dalits, which very powerfully challenge the national consciousness and plead the cause of Dalits. There is the need of broadening and consolidating these trends. Now, many leaders are championing the cause of Dalits and there are Dalit parties. However, they are neither better nor worse than other political parties. Leadership is as corrupt as the general leadership. Parties are personality-based and lack inner-party democracy like any other party. The same prevalent culture of patron-client relationship is maintained in these parties. It would be better for the democracy in the country if Dalits pay attention to the state of affairs in the parties which are primarily based on their support. The Dalits must move from mobilizational political grouping to the associational groupings.

There is the need of thorough caution while accepting liberalization. The vested interests are naturally inclined to subvert the process as they did with the democratic project. It was they who destroyed even the limited potential of the government planned and executed socialism in India. Such subversive acts and at the same time all the disastrous policies of the government and the malicious machinations of the powers that be and their cronies resulting in general miseries and social dislocations are blamed on liberalization. One must exercise extreme caution and must be beware of spurious scholarships and phoney journalistic analyzes which cloud our consciousness by their abundance.

There is also the possibility that government follows a growth model without working for equity in society. Nationwide gross neglect of education and health services indicate to the dangerous trend.[26] There is gross deterioration in such basic services so fundamental for equity in society, not to speak of the larger enabling role of the government, whereas the need of the hour is to augment efforts in this direction. Such trend would increase social inequality and inequity further and thus limiting the effects of liberalization. The democratic movements must pressurize the government to strengthen education. Their lost functionality and prestige are in dire need for restoration. The government must be compelled to work for the revival of government schools, colleges and even universities and should encourage philanthropy, voluntary and cooperative efforts and facilitate private and foreign players in the field. Education is not only the most powerful medium of empowerment and social mobility but is empowerment by itself. Simultaneously, the government must spend more on sports and cultural activities along the length and breadth of the country and facilitate, i.e., remove the roadblocks in the way of voluntary and private players. In India, what is needed is a combination of the growth model and the anthropocentric models of development. The unrestrained entrepreneurship must be combined with massive investments in people, i.e., in physical and social infrastructure. There should not be any constraint of resources in this regard. There is huge possibility of mobilizing resources by pruning the government expenditures (mostly unnecessary but incurred for the benefit of powers that be) in other areas and by divesting the public sector holdings. Further, huge resources can be channelled in this area simply by removing constraints on investments from the corporate sector. Such idealism treating education as selfless service or non-profit public responsibility is bogus and counterproductive. Such idealism is good; the inclined parties must follow such idealism but that cannot be made the rule. Disallowing the commercialization of education is something highly irrational. Commercialization is must for expansion and improvement of educational facilities in our country. Otherwise, education will remain the fiefdom of crooks, politicians and bureaucrats. Whoever castigates the private educational institutions as teaching shops must know that the government ones are PDS shops which do not stock what is needed and stock what is rotten. One must know that profit is a very legitimate motive; motives other than profit (so flaunted) are mostly fraudulent.

Recently, the liberalization efforts, though lackadaisical, have ensured plenty of jobs in the market. Even foreigners are flocking in the country to seek employment. This is the main factor for rising salaries which ultimately threatens India's cost competitiveness in the international market. And, at the same time, there remains large-scale unemployment in the country (around 9%). Problem is that there is a dearth of skilled manpower.[27] While economy has been opened considerably, the education sector is still under the influence of the Brahmanic-socialistic mindsets which inhibit the corporatization of the education sector. The government sector education is while abysmally lacking in quality also does not meet the quantity requirements. And moreover, the government/government controlled education system is not attuned to the needs of the market. This has resulted in the dearth of skilled manpower on one side and presence of large-scale unemployment on the other. The market economy even in such a short span of time and despite so much dithering on the part of the government is fulfiling its promise but is hampered by the failings of the government even in its primary jobs—providing education in this case. Now, while opening of the education sector has become inevitability under GATS, and the better days for the sector appears on the horizon, the government has expanded and extended its reservation policy not only to the government institutions including institutions of excellence like IITs and IIMs but also to private and foreign educational institutions. And if private players are allowed to get in even with manageable fetters the decline of even IITs and IIMs would not be that tragic. These institutions excelled only partially because of liberal funding, good infrastructure and relative autonomy ensured to them (under the same showcasing model of development) but substantially because they attracted the créme-de-la-créme of the one-fifth of humanity as there were no options. Let the government spoil institutions they own; taxpayers must get penalized for electing wrong persons in power or supporting wrong policies out of their ignorance. But not at any cost, private players should be penalized, nor should they be coerced into charity. Such measures create multilayered distortions in their operations which harm the interest of the players, the customers and the nation. And, one should never forget that reservation is not a substitute for the failures of human development policies, it is part of the gimmickry in the name of human development. Moreover, the basic fact should never be forgotten that notwithstanding temporary alterations, there should not be heavy overlapping or usurpation of jobs in society. Welfare is a job which belongs to the voluntary sector; the main job of market is to ensure profit for the participants; government is there to guarantee contracts which include the social contract between the government and the civil society binding the former to ensure the safety of life, liberty and property of the latter.

At the same time, any set of depressed individuals must not fall prey to lofty idealism which ultimately serves no purpose except leading to the change of ruling classes. All efforts and sacrifices go in vain while people move from one form of bondage to another. One must identify the right kind of idea or ideology. An ideology is sound only when it espouses generalized democratic culture which favours all and disfavours none. In the beginning of the last decade, the Dalits supported the implementation of the MandaI Commission in the hope of getting a better deal but that proved illusive. In the words of Chandra Bhan Prasad, a Dalit ideologue, "The MandaI counter-revolution set an altogether different agenda—replacing Brahmin hegemony by a new hegemony of intermediary castes, OBCs to be precise. Dalits failed to understand the Mandal logic: In challenging Brahmin hegemony, OBCs present themselves as victims. Dalits as landless were a handy tool. No wonder then, the first massacre of Dalits in north India occurred in Belchi in May 1977, immediately after the Janata Party came to power. The first massacre of Dalits in Tamil Nadu occurred in December 1968 shortly after the DMK came to power. In Kilvenmani village, 44 Dalits were burnt alive. Since then, in south and north, such massacres have evolved into a new form of social assertion."[28] And this is not an aberration. In fact, caste movement in Tamil Nadu is the oldest but the lot of Dalits has hardly improved there; they are still oppressed.

Liberalization, thus, has the potential to atomize the society to single individuals. Atomized society where every person is judged by his/her ability and contribution she can make to the economy is antithetical to the ascribed roles and status. Liberalization also maximizes social mobility. Nonetheless, there are apprehensions with regard to liberalization but are not well-founded. Opposition to liberalization arises mainly because of the socialization process of the socialist days when socialistic indoctrination had vitiated the curricula of schools and colleges. The colonial psychic fear of the East India Company capturing India also plays its role notwithstanding the fact that India today is the second largest investing country in the United Kingdom. Moreover, the Datit scholarship has also a role to play in such kind of approach. Broadly their writing reflects anguish over inhuman treatment meted out to them which is very natural and legitimate. Their achievements despite so much socio-economic odds is nothing but praiseworthy and their pride is fully deserved. However, in the absence of a suitable theoretical paradigm, they adopt *liftism* as their tool of understanding and reflection. This is the reason for vociferous protests against liberalization. However, this does not alter the fact that even today Dalits are socially challenged. Their problem is not poverty alone but that their attempts to improve their living conditions are resisted by dominant local castes. In fact, liberalization not only provides opportunities for entrepreneurship and employment but also dismantles caste as the basis of socio-political groupings. This is evident from the way people organize themselves in the post-modern cities like Bangalore or in suburbs like Gurgoan where professionals and resident welfare associations have started assuming political roles for the better management of their surroundings. The challenge to Dalits comes mainly from traditional settings, agrarian communities or cities which are extensions of agrarian economies. In modern and post-modern cities (read industrial and knowledge economy-based cities respectively), the caste congregations in terms of residential locality or menial/unclean jobs may be continuing but they are not bothered or oppressed on the basis of caste considerations. From there they can build up on as these places throw open immense opportunities. If liberalizationis rooted, that means private property gets the sanctity it deserves, that is to say property rights and their religious protection becomes the central focus of the whole political organization, no person can be held back if he has the desire to move.

Notes

1. A survey conducted by global human resource services firm Hewitt noted that India in 2005 witnessed an average salary hike of 14.1 per cent—the highest in the world. Cited in T.R. Vivek, "Money for keeps", *Outlook,* April 3, 2006, p. 82.
2. The poverty rate has declined from 54.9 per cent in 1973–74 to 26.1 per cent in 1999–2000. Data cited in *Outlook,* April 3, 2006, p. 80.
3. The author has got this impression from his interactions with Dalits—colleagues and others, different reports and writings in newspapers and magazines and submissions in various seminars. However, for instance one can see Kancha Ilaiah, "Buffalo Nationalism: A Critique of Spiritual Fascism," *Samaya,* Kolkata, 2004, pp. 155–168.
4. Arun Prabha Mukherjee, "Introdution" (by the translator), *Joothan: A Dalit's Life,* by Omprakash Valmiki, Trans. Arun Prabha Mukherjee, Kolkata: *Samaya,* 2003, pp. xi-xii.
5. For the concept of substantialization see, Susan Bayly, *Caste, Society and Politics in India: From the Eighteenth Century to the Modern Age,* Cambridge University Press, 1999, pp. 309–311.
6. Chandra Bhan Prasad, "In Search of A Dalit Bourgeoisie", *The Times of India,* the late city edition, August 9, 2005.
7. Such sentiments are commonplace among Dalits. For instance the Lok Sabha Deputy Speaker, S.S. Atwal, and former President, K.R. Narayanan expressed similar sentiments in a national summit of Dalit organizations. Narayanan blamed that 'unrestricted globalization and privatization' were taking away reservations for Dalits and tribes. Similar sentiments were expressed by Deputy Speaker Atwal. Strongly advocating the demand for reservation in private sector, he warned that there were social forces plotting to take away existing reservation provisions from SCs/STs. "Had there not been reservation, I would not have been a deputy speaker and there would not have been so many Dalits in top positions", he said. *The Times of India,* ""Dalits raise demand for quota in private sector", New Delhi, the late city edition, August 11, 2005.
8. Bipan Chandra, Mridula Mukherjee and Aditya Mukherjee, *India After Independence: 1947–2000,* Penguin Books India, New Delhi, 1991, pp. 364–365.
9. *The Economic Times,* "Corporates that Care: A Special Feature on Corporate Social Responsibility", January, 18 2006.

   —, "Corporates that Care: A Special Feature on Corporate Social Responsibility", Part II, March, 17 2006.
10. The issue can be understood for instance by the sentiments expressed by Adi Godrej, the leading industrialist of India, "We, as the older generation, are stupid to have believed in socialism". The sentiments stemmed from the fact that it was the licence raj and babudom coupled with high

taxation in the 70's and 80's that deterred Godrej from growing his company the way he wanted to, the way he sees Reliance and Infosys grow today. "Today's entrepreneurs can think freely, think big and think confidently" he said. Sudeshna Chatterjee, "Captain Courageous", *Times Life* (Sunday supplement of the *Times of India*), March 10, 2006, p. 1 and 3.

11. Ambedkar was a pioneer of such a vision and as a political activist, social reformer and as member of the Constituent Assembly and as president of drafting committee, he tried to impact the system with this perspective. For instance, see H.S. Dwivedi and Ratan Sinha, "Dr Ambedkar: The Pioneer of Social Democracy", *The Indian Journal of Political Science*, Vol. LXXVI, No. 3, July-September 2005, pp. 661–666.
12. Chandra Bhan Prasad, "The Empire Strikes Back", *The Times of India*, New Delhi, the late city edition, September 7, 2005.
13. For the concept of sanskritization, see M.N. Srinivas, *Social Change in Modern India*, 1966.
14. M.N. Srinivas, "An Obituary on Caste as a System", *Economic and Political Weekly*, Vol. XXXVIII, No. 5, February 1–7, 2003, p. 455.
15. Ibid., p. 457.
16. For instance, a study of rural Punjab by Jodhka can be cited. Dalits there have asserted their social and cultural position through what Jodhka terms as the strategies of 'disassociation, distancing and autonomy'. They are growingly disassociating with 'unclean' jobs and if they do such things, they do not do so not in the framework of jajmani ties. Secondly, they have started distancing themselves from agricultural labour, despite being landless, because of their acute dislike of the dependency relationship with the farmer than the nature of the work. To quote Jodhka's observation, "However, such a distancing is possible only where alternative sources of them employment become available to them. The opening of the village economy and its growing linkage with towns has made it physically possible for them to look out to other sources of employment, and many of have been doing precisely that." As for the third strategy, Jodhka writes, "For living a life of dignity, they need their own autonomous cultural resources ... . Wherever, they could mobilize resources, the Dalits of Punjab have tried to construct their own gurudwaras and other local level institutions in order to attain a certain degree of cultural autonomy from the dominant castes." All these three strategies indicate to the crucial role played by the opportunities available to the Dalits outside villages or became available to them by the opening of village economies. Surinder S. Jodhka, "Caste and Untouchablity in Rural Punjab", *Economic and Political Weekly*, Vol. XXXVII, No. 19, May 11–17, 2002, pp. 1813–1823.
17. Manimala, (ed.), *Jeet Lenge Andhere Ko: Dalit Mahila Netritva Ek Safar*, (Hindi), New Delhi: Books for Change, 2004.

18. *The Times of India,* "Castes of Mind", New Delhi, the late city edition, September 3, 2005.
19. M.N. Srinivas, No. 14, p. 459.
20. *India Today,* March 27, 2006, p. 43.
21. Frangois Bourguignon and Shantayanan Devarajan, "All that you can't leave behind: Growth bandwagon cannot afford to exclude the poor", *The Times of India,* New Delhi, the late city edition, September 24, 2005.
22. Arindam Mukherjee, "Miss World: Bold, brash and going where no MNC has gone before .... Indian companies make their presence felt globally", *Outlook,* April 3, 2006, p. 88.19.
23. In fact, the very struggle for social justice and human dignity as it started in South India (Madras Presidency) under the leadership of Ramasamy Naicker was based on the rejection of religion and godhood. Though the movement went haywire, a very powerful precedent is there. For reference the article can be seen, A.P.S. Chouhan and Niraj Kumar Jha, "Periyar: Persona, Principles, Praxis", *The Indian Journal of Political Science,* Vol. LXXVI, No. 3, July-September 2005, pp. 667–692.
24. Ibid.
25. *The Times of India,* "Dismiss Hooda, say Dalit leaders", New Delhi, the late city edition, September 6, 2005.
26. The problematic part is not only that the government spends less on health and education (0.91% of GDP on health and 4.1% of GDP on education as cited in Anu Aga, "Inverted Pyramid", *Outlook,* April 3, 2006, p. 80.) but also that the most of the allocations are wasted and siphoned off by the concerned bureaucracy. People do not visit government hospitals or enroll their kids in government schools if they can afford not to do so. Even government colleges and universities are out of sync with times and have become white elephants.
27. *Dainik Bhaskar* Sunday, "Dus Saal Men Tees Lakh Ko Naukari", Gwalior (Hindi Daily), March 12, 2006, p. 1.
28. Chandra Bhan Prasad, p. 12.

4

Incredulity towards 'Metanarrative' and Dalit Politics

AKHILESH KUMAR SHARMA

This paper tries to interpret Dalit politics by locating it within the politics of resistance that is characterized by, to borrow the Leotardian phrase, an 'incredulity towards metanarratives'. In the globalization era, one of the implications of this skepticism towards metanarratives has been a quest for different modes of representation predicated upon skepticism, if not a summary rejection of abstract categories like 'class' and 'state'. Rooted in 'everyday', there is a more generalized emphasis on 'here', 'now' and 'everyday'.[1]

The Politics of Resistance

It may here be pointed out that some of the major critiques of globalization have emanated not from some universal ideological formulations but from some loosely knit coalitions working for environment, farmers, pacifism and trade unionism. Activists who marched in the frontline in Seattle were from Earth First, Alliance for Sustainable Jobs and Environment, Food not Bombs, Global Exchange and the Ruckus Society, and a vocal contingent of French farmers.[2]

Different from the earlier resistances, they are not fixed to any particular place and their strength lies in their not being fixated over time and place as well as their strength and capacity to confront the forces of global capital across the globe. Also, as loose coalitions, they operate on different terrains. Not having any master narrative of capitalism or anti-capitalism at the base, they may often have contradictory impulses. These movements are marked by a singular absence of any sort of trade unionism—Left or Right. Clairs Seattle's diary notes how after the day first protests and police violence, the labour contingent of the AFL-CIO, that was supposed to join other protestors at the convention centre, didn't turn up because they were promised 'a seat at the table'. Eventually, the more radical among the steelworkers and longshoremen managed to come, revolting against the decision of their leaders.[3] Thus, the distinguishing feature of these resistance movements is their refusal to privilege one particular kind of oppression over others.

Dalit Viewpoints of India

Let us first consider the views expressed by 13 Dalit organizations from Andhra Pradesh. In a memorandum to the President of India, they alleged that the distrust between the 'touchables' and 'untouchables' is also growing.

India is a nation for all its citizens. But to us, the 'quasi-citizens', India is only an idea with a dubious past. Our exclusion was an accepted rule. We were taught to love labour without any fruits … . When India evolved into a republic, it sought to mature into a nation. The two identities, of Dalits and of the others, were to wither away. A civil society was to evolve; a point of convergence was to emerge. Our exclusion was to end … . That goal still remains a dream. The masters of the republic have even stopped dreaming. The dream itself appears to have withered away … . Democracy is a wonderful doctrine. It helps everybody. It helped the West. Democratize ownership patterns. Democratize the workforce of institutions you own … . Call the creators. Rather, invite them … . Accord us our due representation … . Fifty years have passed, our exclusion remains. The two societies remain, with all their divisiveness. Mutual distrust and hatred are growing. The State has done a bit … . Only the State. Because there is a Constitution. Because there was a constitution-maker … . But the society—we mean the private world, where are we? What has it done to us? Who will end this? And when? … Make your private public. Private is not above public. If you import capital and technology from the US, import vision from there as well.[4]

Viewing themselves as quasi-citizens of India, their anguish at the failure of the republic to usher in a nation and a civil society is more discernible. What agonises them more is the fact that the dream—of equal citizenry—itself has been abandoned. It refers to the retreat of the state that implies almost an abandonment of the idea of affirmative action. Democracy, according to the memorandum, does not merely mean the existence of democratic institutions but a democratization of the ownership patterns. However, in the same vein, the document opines that whatever little has been done for them, it has only been done by the state. With the advent of globalization, liberalization, privatization and the consequent retreat of the state, even that little is disappearing fast. But they do not resort to any anti-globalization rhetoric. Rather, they talk of importing vision from the US.

Chandrabhan Prasad elaborated it in a series of articles in his "Dalit Diary", which he wrote in *The Pioneer*. He refers to the Kerner Commission, set-up in the wake of civil rights movement—in the US in 1967, which proposed a host of affirmative action packages for the Blacks. Referring to the creation of the Minority Business Development Agency which was conceived as a nodal body in the US "to assist in the growth of minority business", he goes on to say: "The US government coined the slogan 'Democratic Capital' when it observed: Economic growth can not be sustained without the inclusion of minority business and the infusion of capital into minority business".[5] In a series of articles in his "Dalit Diary", he gives a detailed account of the ways in which these steps have helped in the development of non-white business. He notes the ways in which big private corporations, like the Microsoft and the IBM, have responded to the recruitment of Blacks, the Hispanics and the Native Americans. Among the things that the Microsoft does are: (a) offering a theoretical justification of affirmative action in the private sector; (b) offering of scholarships to the Black! ethnic students and organizing of special training programmes for them; (c) recruiting Black! ethnic people; (d) purchasing materials/goods from Black! ethnic business houses and contractors, and (e) involving itself in community programmes.[6]

This is not to argue that there is something in-built in the American vision that makes such initiatives by the private sector possible. On the contrary, it is the long history of struggle against racial discrimination that created an overall atmosphere for affirmative action to become an imperative even for corporations. Thus, it is not merely a gift of the American state, but a product of prolonged struggle. However, this is not the issue here to go into detail.

It must here be pointed out that in India, not all Dalit intellectuals share this optimism. The primacy accorded to the state is more widely shared. Gopal Guru, for instance, argues that the Indian state, and not the civil society, appears to be their most important benefactor.[7] This is not so only in the context of affirmative action, but also in the context of its role as protector of Dalits in the society where their oppression happens to be the greatest.[8]

But the attitude towards the state notwithstanding, there is no unanimity among them regarding the attitude as to how to view its retreat from the critical sectors of the economy and the society.[9] The following episode may throw some light on why most Dalits might hesitate to draw a straightforward linkage between the former and the latter. In 1993, the Indian People's Front (IPF) organized a convention in New Delhi on a theme related to the challenges of globalization foe, which the Dunkel Draft and the animated opposition that it drew provided the context. One of the speakers representing Dalit Mahasangh voiced a discordant note on the issue of national unity against imperialism. Will it not lead to their marginalization once again? Will not they be yoked into another unity under upper caste leadership forcing them to defer their demands indefinitely just when the Dalits are trying to assert themselves?

The point I am trying to make here is that even when someone like Gopal Guru might not like to throw his lot with the demand for 'democratization of capital', someone like the above-mentioned speaker may not be too willing to join forces for a nationalist mobilization against those of globalization. The only possible course of action for them then appears to be of the type that is advocated by the Dalit organizations' memorandum—of staking their claim in whatever dispensation that emerges.

Nationalist Imagery and the Dalits

Needless to say, most of the Dalit intellectuals pinned their faith in the post-colonial Indian state as their protector and ameliorator. But an interesting paradox needs to be unraveled here. Even during the hey-days of the legitimacy of the post-colonial state, the voices of Dalit as independent actors on the political stage could not emerge in any significant ways. For the phase of state legitimacy was also a phase of Nehruvian secular-nationalist imagery. After independence, the coalition formed by the Congress was essentially composed of upper castes, Muslims and Dalits, with upper caste hegemony. Thus, even within the secular dispensation, the domination of the Hindu upper caste prevailed. Even though, the state might have acted as a kind of relatively benign institution in Dalit defence, albeit half-heartedly, the overall relations of power structure were not disturbed.

That is why scholars like Kancha Ilaiah have even described the Nehruvian state as merely fulfiling a Brahminical agenda of establishing their control over state institutions.[10] Whether one agrees or disagrees with Kancha Ilaiah, there is no denying the fact that the period of a benign role of the state was also a period of upper caste control over it. No doubt, the policy of affirmative action pursued by the state led to the opening up of the state institutions, particularly the administrative services, to the Dalit intelligentsia up to a certain extent, which, in turn, provided a basis for the subsequent political mobilization of the Dalit masses in the eighties. This has been precisely the reason why the state is seen as a benefactor. Moreover, abolition of untouchability and prohibition of discrimination based on caste put a check, though in a limited sense, on blatant caste abuses, especially in urban areas. On the other hand, the 'nation', a legacy of the freedom struggle, came to be understood as representing the domain of the society, because of the predominance of the upper castes in its structures. Almost on a daily basis, it seemed to be subverting the social contract embodied in the Constitution. And while doing so, it also seemed to be subverting the 'nation' of the dream.

But this way of looking at the post-colonial state only partly explains the emergence of autonomous Dalit politics in the 1980s. The political assertion of Dalits in the 80s and 90s is organically linked to the decline of the nationalist imagery, as also to the decline of the Nehruvian state's legitimacy. This decline was followed by the 'insurrection of the little selves', which made possible the articulation of an autonomous Dalit voice.[11] And when Kanshi Ram coined this slogan in the 1990s "hamein mazboot sarkar nahin, mazboor sarkar chahiye", it merely reflected an urge for the rejection of the nationalist desire for political stability and order. At a deeper level, it suggests that the state is not the Constitution. On the contrary, it represents a condensation of power relations existing in the society at large. It may also be seen as an understanding of the dialectic of power wherein the constitutional mandate of that state can be seen to co-exist in an uneasy truce with the Brahminical predominance of Nehruvian secular nationalism.

Thus, nationalism and secularism of the Nehruvian variety basically remained an upper caste Hindu discourse in so far as it remained indifferent to the non-secular discriminations of the past. By prohibiting the articulation of challenges to power that was expressed in non-secular languages of caste and community, the state willy-nilly preserved the predominant position of the Brahminical elite. This elite, which gained control over the institutions of the state structure, was not willing to relinquish its control over the assets and institutions of the society. It is not surprising, therefore, that Kanshi Ram, the man behind weaving together of a Bahujan political identity, understood that this nationalist desire for unity and stability was also a desire for 'continuity' of Dalit exploitation.

Thus, Dalits do not see towards the state as unproblematically to be their benefactor. They also view the continuation of their social oppression in it. And, that is why their attempt to chart out a different course of action in face of the challenges of globalization. It is not surprising, therefore, that the Dalit political leaders and intellectuals are not willing to throw their lot behind the call for halting the juggernaut of globalization in defence of the state.

Thus, what emerges from the above discussion is a refusal on the part of Dalits to countenance any metanarrative of their emancipation. Often, they represent a desire to address different oppressions together. However, this should not lead us to a conclusion that a united nationalist movement against the globalization juggernaut is not possible. It may only be possible when the more immediate issues concerning Dalits are also taken into account rather than expect them to abandon their own issues and join the mainstream. There is a need to realize that those who live on the margins have different kinds of pressures to cope with and different perceptions of the set of problems that they face in their daily lives.

Notes

1. Globalization is a combination of processes such as transnationalization of capital, information technology revolution, environmentalism, collapse of socialism and consequent skepticism towards universalist discourses of emancipation.
2. Jeffrey St. Clair, "Seattle Diary: It's a Gas, Gas, Gas", *New Left Review*, 238, November-December 1999.
3. Ibid.
4. Chandrabhan Prasad, 'P.S.: Where are the Visionaries?' in "Dalit Dairy", *The Pioneer*, January 28, 2001.
5. Chandrabhan Prasad, 'Righting Wrongs, the American Way', in "Dalit Diary", *The Pioneer*, February 4, 2001.
6. Ibid.
7. His paper presented in a seminar on "Dalits, Liberalization and the State", organized by the Punjab University in May 2001.
8. Gopal Guru, "Dalits in Pursuit of Modernity", in Romila Thapar (ed.), *India-Another Millenium*? (New Delhi: Viking Penguin Books, 2000).
9. Gopal Guru and V. Geetha, "New Phase of Dalit-Bahujan Intellectual Activity", *Economic and Political Weekly*, January 15, 2000.
10. Kancha Ilaiah, "Towards the Dalitization of the Nation", in Partha Chatterjee (ed.), *Wages of Freedom: Fifty Years of the Indian Nation State* (Delhi: Oxford University Press, 1998).
11. Aditya Nigam, "Secularism, Modernity, Nation: Epistemology of the Dalit Critique", *Economic and Political Weekly*, November 25, 2000.

5

Revisiting Dalitism in the Global Age

LOKESH K. PRASAD

In order to conceptualize the term 'Dalit', it may be pointed out that it is directly linked to a perception of deprivation. It literally means 'to be trampled upon. The term is coined by Bhim Rao Ambedkar, one of the founding fathers of the Indian Constitution, to signify that segment of the society who are systematically and institutionally deprived of their civil, political, economic, social and cultural rights in every aspect of life. They occupy the lowest rung in the caste hierarchy and they are subjected to extreme forms of social and economic exclusion and discrimination, such as, denial to access to land, forced to work in degrading conditions and routinely abused by higher-caste groups. They fall outside the hierarchy of the fourfold varna/caste system based on the concept of purity and pollution. They are categorized as 'ati-shudras', and they are considered far too polluting to be within the varna system. They have historically been allocated occupations that are considered demeaning or polluting by others.

At independence, however, India's new democratic republic provided them equal status in the caste hierarchy of the Indian society. The Indian Constitution, based on the principles of equality, liberty and justice, made it mandatory for the reinterpretation of the caste system to accommodate egalitarian values. Notwithstanding, in the initial years, caste continued to be associated with cumulative inequalities of status, income and power. But as the institutions of

Indian democracy matured, the socio-political and economic conditions of Dalits too, changed for, their betterment which brought them into the mainstream of the Indian society. However, it still needs a lot more to be done in this regard. For this, it is important that the efforts in this direction should be all-comprehensive and conclusive in order to attain their all-round development, especially in the rural India.

The structure of the discussion is as follows: Section I examines the issue of inequalities in the context of the systemic change in the erstwhile socialist countries. Section II deals with the question of unequals in the Indian society in relation to caste dominance, alongwith the new demographic trends which are gradually, but steadily, emerging in the rural India. Section III provides a new interpretation to the concept of social justice in post-reform India. Section IV evaluates the issue of reservation in the light of recent debate between legislature and judiciary. Section V draws together some conclusions.

I
Global Change: Issue of Inequalities

The last decade of the 20th century witnessed a remarkable politico-economic transformation across the world. The winds of change blew over the communist states so suddenly and effectively that it caught the rest of the world unaware. Various scholars have described this phenomenal change differently. Francis Fukuyama named it 'the end of history'.[1] Ngaire Woods described it as the emergence of the 'borderless world'.[2] For Samuel P. Huntington, this systemic change was the 'third wave' of democratization.[3] James N. Rosenau viewed it as the 'legitimacy crisis in authoritarian regimes'.[4] Still, for John Nasbitt it is the transition towards 'market democracy'[5] and some relates it to the theory of the 'end of ideology'.[6] But, the crux of the matter is that the spread of polyarchy in the former communist states was due to the worsening global conditions combined with the inability of the command economics to reform adequately, brought their economic difficulties to a new stage in the 1980s. These socialist governments failed to meet the rising social and economic expectations of the general populace.[7]

Consequent upon this, rapid and far-reaching political changes took place in the communist countries in 1989. For one country after another, the ruling Communist Party was forced to renounce its monopoly in politics and society and negotiate the transition to substantially altered political and economic structures. Although the interdependence among these developments was striking, from a global perspective Central and East European countries and, in 1991, the Soviet Union were among the last hold-outs in the 'third wave' of democratization that had started in the middle of 1970.

According to Samuel P. Huntington, the first wave started in the USA in 1820s and ended after 1926. The second wave began in the early 1940s and ended at the beginning of the 1960s.[8] The 'third wave' of change began in southern Europe in the mid-1970s when dictatorship in Greece, Portugal and Spain relinquished power. In 1983, a three-year long military intervention ended in Turkey. In Africa and Latin America, too, authoritatarian regimes veered towards politico-economic liberalization in order to gain internal support for policies necessitated by their deepening economic crisis. By the mid-1980s, all the South American military formations except those in Chile and Paraguay had retreated to the barracks, and by 1990 they too followed suit. In the 1980s, transition began in a number of Asian countries including South Korea, Pakistan, the Philippines, Taiwan, Thailand and India (1991). At the end of the decade, the economic crisis led to the collapse of communist regimes and speeding up of economic liberalization in these economies.

The spread of polyarchy in the late 1980s was of a different nature from the democratic shift in the 1970s and 1980s. In the latter case, the events themselves were relatively independent, at least among those countries where a shift from right wing, often military based regimes occurred. The goals were limited to maintenance of power and the implementation of selective policies. In the setting of communist systems, however, the aim was implementation of an alternative form of political, social and economic development, that is, a stateless and classless society. The failure of this effort was evident all over the communist world. Communism collapsed as the result of long-term processes of regional change which came to fruition in the late 1980s. In Hungary and Poland, the changes were evolutionary, whereas in the rigid, conservative regimes in Bulgaria, Czechoslovakia and East Germany evolutionary momentum was completely lacking. In these countries noted for elite intransigence, changes occurred rapidly. In Poland and Hungary, by contrast factions within the communist parties opened up channels of communication with the opposition, thus facilitating a more gradual change.

James N. Rosenau viewed the politico-economic change in the beginning of 1990s as the legitimacy crisis of authoritarian regimes.[9] In addition to the Gorbachev factor, he cited "the impact of technology, the consequences of new interdependence issues, the advent of authority crisis, and the greater competence of sub-groups and citizens" as major contributory factors for changes in the communist regimes and elsewhere. J.F. Brown points to six interrelated causes that reflect some of these themes in the specific setting of eastern Europe: forty years of failure, in particular economic failure, illegitimacy of communism, societal opposition, the loss of confidence in the ability to rule and the accompanying unwillingness to apply means to force to maintain rule, improvement in East-West relations, and finally, the Soviet factor.[10]

The question arose of the legitimacy of communism in modern societies. According to Rosenau, the erosion of ideology increasingly forced the communist regimes to base their right to rule on socio-economic criteria. It became commonplace to explain past compliance of the people in the region with common in terms of the delivery of certain social and economic benefits, a sort of 'social contract'.[11] But once the communist regimes linked their legitimacy to the provision of material resources, economic and political reforms became indispensable. If these reforms did not result in visible economic development, the dominant party risked population mistrust.

The worsening global economic conditions combined with the inability of the command economics to reform adequately, brought their economic difficulties to a new stage in the 1980s. The need to meet rising social and economic expectations contributed to economic and political liberalization in most of the communist countries, the efforts at legitimization shifting gradually from the economic to the political sphere.

Various scholars have acknowledged that "failure of most of the communist regimes to establish or retain political authority, that is, to win the acknowledgement of the populations that the regimes had a right to rule"[12] was a primary cause of the collapse of communism. The upheavals in eastern Europe in the fall of 1989 were the 'mass action of unhappy people'.[13] Authoritarian regimes base their power on the servitude and discipline of their officials, civilian and military, 'the non-deviant actors of society'[14] but an ageing leadership proved incapable of responding to new and challenging demands. In the absence of institutionalized channels for appointing leaders to meet the needs of the times *gerontocratic leadership* became a marked feature of socialist societies. Thus, Todor Zhivkov had been at the helm of the Bulgarian Communist Party since 1954, Janos Kadar had been in the leadership position in Hungary since 1956, Nicolae Ceausescu had led the Romanian Workers Party since 1965, Gustav Husak had became First Secretary in Czechoslovakia in 1969, and Erich Honecker had succeeded Walter Ulbricht in 1971.[15] In 1988, they still retained their posts.

Among the masses, the feelings of socio-economic deprivation and disillusionment with the communist system had deepened. Professional and social mobility was low with upward channels of mobility limited to selected elite. Self-recruitment and not competition, became a distinctive feature of society. The living standard of the general population was characterized by relatively small income differentials. In addition, the assortment of goods available lacked quality, services and infrastructure were inadequate, and the masses had limited travel possibilities. The reduction of inequalities, which enabled the ruling elite to cling to power, also undermined their power base, since efficiency, innovation and development had been paralyzed. The relative high levels of quality confined to a limited few contrasted sharply with the extreme inequality in the access to and use of power. Socialism, thus had achieved 'an equality of injustice'.[16]

Overall, it may be commented that the imperatives of socio-economic modernization ultimately led to political democratization but not necessarily system transformation, albeit 'gradually through incremental changes'. However, this remarkable geographic diffusion of the liberal democratic state also paved way for inequalities in income and wealth distribution arising out of the relationship between the recent geographic expansion of democracy and the economic phenomenon of globalization. Despite the institutions of global governance and liberal democracy, the world remains divided as ever into the rich and poor countries.[17] According to the United Nations World Development Report, 1996 the world is divided in where the richest 358 people owned as much wealth as the poorest two and a half billion.[18]

Moreover, the developing countries have experienced unprecedented decline in price and volume of their exports excluding petroleum. They have accumulated more than $1 trillion international debt. They are experiencing a reverse transfer of resources in order to service their debts. In addition, the economic aid and other assistance to them, be it bilateral or multilateral, has been subjected to various conditions. These include economic as well as non-economic factors, such as human rights, press freedom, defence expenditure, etc. Their collective bargaining spirit has collapsed. Instead of cooperation, they are clearly divided on account of their differing expectations from international cooperation. In fact, there has emerged a selective coalition and partnership of developing countries with developed countries. Moreover, almost all of them have come under the structural adjustment programmes of the IMF and the World Bank. They have liberalized their economies under these programme and have opened their economies for more trade and investment.[19] In fact, while developed countries have been restraining imports from developing countries by various measures, the developing countries have increasingly been under pressure by the IMF, the World Bank and the bilateral donors to open their economies for trade and investment.

Empirically, Susan Strange, in her study of South East and East Asian 'tiger' economies, established that the new competitiveness in these economies have not been able to free themselves from their dependency on the centre in the now more important field of services. Despite their export drive, these economics are obviously dependent on outlets for export led industrialization in the more advanced countries. The latter reacts to these additional export with "strategies of oligopolistic behaviour based on power relations".[20] However, the concept of 'continued dependency' has been opposed on the ground that the more advanced countries would be inefficient in this endeavour as the regulatory powers of states are on decline, despite monopoly.[21]

II

Question of Unequals in the Indian Context

In India, the term 'Dalit' has a direct linkage with the issue of inequalities. It has its basis in the hereditary caste groups which are placed in a position of ritual superiority or inferiority to the others. Varna refers to the four universal unchanging categories of the Hindu hierarchy—Brahmin, Kshatriya, Vaisha and Sudra—which are common to all areas of India and provide an overarching ritual ranking system. In pre-modern times, rigorous criteria of pollution and purity has restricted even the rudiments of education to the children of the 'twice-born' castes, that is, the Brahmin, Kshatriya, and Vaisha varnas. On contrary, the Sudras, the most numerous of the four varna strata, including the peasantry and members of artisan had to be content with opportunities for pursuing their own spiritual merit through service of these superior castes. At the bottom of the religious hierarchy, moreover, one in five persons had no varna standing at all. They were considered so unclean as to defile caste persons merely by touch, or in some extreme cases, by sight. They were considered as outcastes or 'untouchables' who were engaged in menial and indispensable services.[22]

In modern times, the varna hierarchy were still the guiding factor for allocating religious and ritual rights and obligations among the multitude of caste groups. Occasionally, locally dominant Sudra caste might be able to establish a claim to higher varna rank after changing group customs, religious ritual and style of life in imitation of an elite caste. But, this process of 'sanskritization'[23] as a vehicle for social mobility was a prolonged one, extending over one or two generations and it led only to positional changes within the local hierarchy. Notwithstanding, the principles of the hierarchical varna order and the structure of local infidelity remained essentially unchanged.

During the British period, the caste structure was challenged by the secular norms of equality, liberty and justice, such as, equality before the law, etc. The desire for social mobility outside the traditional system was most clearly evident in the Backward Classes Movement of the 1920s and1930s, which had its greatest appeal in the Brahmin-dominated area of the south.[24] These movements were led by powerful peasant-castes succeeded in gaining British support for caste quotas in admission to colleges and places in the civil service, breaking the monopoly of the small South Indian Brahmin community over these posts, mainly in coastal areas and towns. However, as in the case of 'sanskritization', the fruits of Westernization rarely reached the 'untouchable' and other low castes in the local rural hierarchy. Nevertheless, in the most rural areas, the legitimacy of the traditional norms of unequal, albeit, reciprocal rights and obligations was not effectively challenged.

In independent India, caste continued to be associated with cumulative inequalities of status, income and power. But, the varna hierarchy did not provide the only basis, for the actual status ranking of particular local castes. The local caste hierarchy is closely associated with the role of 'dominant landowning castes'. The allocation of political authority, that is, exercise of power and authority, is greatly influenced by the largest landowners among the locally dominant castes.[25]

Apart from these, the new trends of local caste dominance has emerged which is not solely associated with the land owning capacity of caste. Rather, the increase in the monetary capacity of any local caste due to involvement in other professions, such as, business, contractors, etc., has provided a new trend in the local caste dominance. Moreover, the unemployed rural youths also play a prominent role in the local caste dominance. The measures adopted by them is quite alarming as they engaged themselves in anti-social activities, such as kidnapping, murder, extortion, gang-war over government tenders, etc., to establish their caste dominance in the local areas. In addition, they play prominent role in local level politics, that is, in elections of the candidates for panchayats and even influence the outcomes of the elections. The reason for this trend is adequately linked to the growth of the rural landless households. Table 1 shows the percentage of rural households which were 'landless' (owning less than 0.002 ha) and 'near landless' (owing between 0.002 ha and 0.200 ha).

Table 1

Rural Landless Households

Year	*Landless (Households owning less than 0.002 ha)*	*Near Landless (Households owning between 0.002 ha and 0.200 ha)*	*Total*
1960–61	11.68	26.22	37.90
1970–71	9.64	27.78	37.42
1981–82	11.33	28.60	39.93
1991–92	11.25	31.15	42.40

Source: National Sample Survey 17th, 26th and 48th Rounds.

Table 2

Distribution of Owned Holdings

(per cent of total holdings and total area)

Year	*Marginal (< 1ha)*		*Small (1 to 2 ha)*		*Semi-Medium (2 to 4 ha)*		*Medium (14 to 10 ha)*		*Large (10 ha and above)*	
	Holding	*Area*	*Holding*	*Area*	*Holding*	*Area*	*Holding*	*Area*	*Holding*	*Area*
1960–61	60.60	7.59	15.16	12.40	12.86	20.54	9.07	31.23	2.85	28.24
1970–71	62.62	9.76	15.49	14.68	11.40	21.92	7.83	30.73	2.12	22.91
1981–82	66.64	12.22	14.70	16.49	10.78	23.38	6.45	29.83	1.42	18.07
1981–92	69.38	16.93	21.75	33.97	5.06	17.63	2.84	17.64	0.95	13.83

Source: V.M. Rao, in R. Radhakrishna. et al., *India in a Globalizing World: Some Aspects of Macroeconomy, Agriculture and Poverty* (Academic Foundation, New Delhi, 2006), p. 467.

It is significant to note that the era of liberalization began in India with over 40 per cent of rural households being landless or near landless. The proportion of the latter category shows a modest but steady increase since the beginning of the Green Revolution in the early seventies. It would be easy to appreciate the significance of this trend when it is considered alongwith the trend in the distribution of ownership holding.[26]

III
Social Justice in India: A New Interpretation

In the light of the changing socio-politico-economic perspectives in India due to liberalization process since 1991, the concept of social justice requires a new interpretation. The first step towards social justice is evident in Article 17 of the Indian Constitution, which says, 'untouchability' is abolished and its practice in any form is forbidden. It has been assumed that the word 'untouchability' has a well known connotation, primarily referring to any social practice which look down upon certain depressed classes solely on account of their birth and disables them from having any kind of intercourse with people belonging to the so called higher classes or castes.[27] In addition, the Indian Constitution has included safeguards for the advancement of the backward classes amongst the residents of India so that the country may be ensured of all-round development. A major section of such backward classes has been specified in the Constitution as scheduled castes and scheduled tribes because their backwardness is patent. Furthermore, there is a general directive in Article 46 that the state shall promote with special care, the educational and economic interests of the weaker sections of the people, and in particular of the scheduled castes and the scheduled tribes, and shall protect them from social injustice and all forms of exploitation. Besides, there are temporary provisions for special representation of and reservation of seats for the SCs and the STs. Still further, the Constitution has made separate provisions for the amelioration and advancement of all 'backward classes', in general. But, the Constitution does not define 'backward classes'.[28] As such, the simple test for classifying a class as backward may be had from Article 15(4), viz., whether the members of such class are socially and educationally worse off than the rest of the citizens, whether they belong to the scheduled castes or not.[29] Both social and educational backwardness must co-exist for this purpose. First, social backwardness is the ultimate analysis, the result of poverty and may be aggravated by caste. But a classification based solely on caste would be bad.[30] Second, educational backwardness, broadly, speaking, means that the average of student population in the particular class of citizens is below the state average.[31]

Here, it may be argued that the notion of inequalities is closely associated with 'backwardness', both socially and educationally. But, given the magnitude of inequalities in which class, caste, race and gender are interwoven in new ways we encounter a whole new set of problems in conceptualizing justice. In the era of globalization, migration of people across states, market flows and information flows have altered definitions of legitimacy, democracy and the state. Justice in the global age has tended to focus narrowly on political justice and human rights and less attention has been given to the question of social and economic justice.

In the Indian context, the question of social and economic justice is directly linked to the problem of poverty—the main measuring yardsticks for any sort of 'backwardness'. The moral debate on socio-economic justice suggests: how to empower the poor? Table 3 provides the estimates of incidence of poverty in India. It shows that approximately 260 million are poor in 1999–2000. Amongst Dalits out of approximately 160 million, 64 million (40%) of them fall below the poverty line. Therefore, the non-Dalit poors are approximately 196 million which consists of other backward classes and general category.[32]

Table 3

Estimates of Incidence of Poverty in India

Year	*Poverty Ratio (per cent)*			*Number of Poor (million)*		
	Rural	*Urban*	*Combined*	*Rural*	*Urban*	*Combined*
1973–74	56.4	49.0	54.9	261.3	60.0	321.3
1977–78	53.1	45.2	51.3	264.3	64.6	328.9
1983	45.7	40.8	44.5	252.0	70.9	322.9
1987–88	39.1	38.2	38.9	231.9	75.2	307.1
1993–94	37.3	32.4	36.0	244.0	76.3	320.3
1999–00	27.1	23.6	26.1	193.2	67.1	260.3

Source: Government of India, 2003, p. 213.

IV
Issue of Reservation: Recent Trends

A nine-judge Constitution bench had recently in the M. Nagaraj case, dealing with reservation and promotional aspects of government jobs, stressed the exclusion of creamy layer, and the capping the limit of 50 per cent on total reservations.[33] In other ways, the 'privileged' among backwards should be kept out of the purview of reservations and they should be substituted by the 'unprivileged' of the so-called high castes/general category[34] in order to achieve a comprehensive social justice. The present trends suggest that quota benefits were being cornered by some powerful segments of the SCs, the STs and the OBCs which deprived the actual beneficiaries for their socio-economic upliftment. The present UPA government, however, disregarding observations of the Apex Court on excluding the creamy layer from the ambit of quota recently cleared 27 per cent quota for all other backward castes (OBCs) in central educational institutions. This act of government is also a sign of the clout wielded by backward caste chieftains in the UPA government. To be more explicit, the vote-bank politics has led to strong consensus among the UPA allies for ensuring quota for creamy layers. The welfare of 'unprivileged' from all sections of the society has been ignored. As a result, a sense of frustration is very common amongst the 'unprivileged' sections of the society, as the fruits of reservation are only benefiting the already 'privileged' sections of the SCs, the STs and the OBCs.

Illustrating the most recent violent protests by Dalits on the eve of 50th death anniversary of B.R. Ambedkar, it may be pointed out that despite their determined effort to secure education and better their lot, Dalits do not seem to be making much headway. The dilemma is that education among Dalits are fast catching up with others but not prosperity.[35] In 1961, barely 10 per cent of India's 64.4 million scheduled caste population could read and write. By 2001, 45 per cent of the SCs were literate, a 4.5 times growth in 40 years. In the same period, for the population as whole, literacy went up from 24.5 per cent to about 54 per cent, just over two times. Between 1995–2003 the growth in enrolment of Dalit students is 14 per cent in primary education as also for the whole population, 60 per cent in secondary education as against 45 per cent for the whole population, and 106 per cent in higher education as against 42 per cent among the total population. In short, equipped with education, Dalits are seeking a better deal. If they still do not get it, there will be more trouble seen against their socio-economic standing which might heightened the sense of frustration.

Table 4

Occupations of Young Males (15 to 35)

Target Groups	*No. of YM*	*Lit.*	*Lab.*	*Agri.*	*UI*	*RJ*	*St.*	*Un.*
Cultivators	57	53	—	28	14	2	8	5
Landless	66	37	37	—	16	1	7	5
Labourers Artisans	27	24	2	1	15	—	5	4
Scheduled Castes	103	73	34	11	30	3	13	12

Notes: YM: Young Males
St.: Students
Lit.: Literates
Un: Unemployed
Lab.: Casual Labour in Villages
RJ: Regular Job
Agri.: Agriculture
UI: Urban Informal

Source: V.M. Rao in R. Radhakrishna et al., *India in a Globalizing World.* (Academic Foundation, New Delhi, 2006), p. 470.

Table 4 reveals that the negligible number are reporting regular jobs as their occupation in different target groups. Also, the relatively large numbers reporting themselves as students and unemployed (20% to 30%) as aspirants waiting for regular jobs. This interpretation seems all the more plausible when we consider the extent of literacy which is quite high (over 70% among SC young workers and 56% among young workers belonging to landless labour household). In addition to the young workers in cultivator households prefer the urban informal sector jobs to casual labour in the village and not a single worker among them reported casual labour in village as their occupation.[36]

The warning signal is that if the young males either unemployed or still continuing as students are finally driven to accept low-status avenues of employment they could become a source of political and social unrest. This may eventually lead to political mobilization and organization of target groups but it is also possible that the unrest merely results in pressures and disruption without any positive impact on the larger society.[37]

The recent wave of violence in Maharashtra in early December 2006 to "avenge the alleged desecration of the statue of Ambedkar in Kanpur is indicative to the fact that 'Dalits' have been made pawns so many time".[38] The protests were also reported from Gujarat, Uttar Pradesh, Madhya Pradesh and Karnataka where public property were damaged. As a matter of fact, the incident started in that state which is going to have the election of state assembly in a near future. On these incidents, an eminent playwright of India has commented, "someone should have been there to restrain them, to make them understand that the desecration of Ambedkar's statue had a political motive. Violence over statues, names, symbols can't become goals. What do you achieve by damaging public property? This will boomerang on you, not on the politicians".[39]

V
Concluding Remarks

To sum up, it may be opined that the premise on which 'Dalitism' is based is that in a society of unequals, gross inequalities make conflict inherent in its foundation. It signifies that the freedom/liberty does not have a universal character in a class divided society; freedom will mean different things to different classes. It establishes a dialectical relationship between the *provision from above* and the *claim from below;* and it strives for the flow from the latter to the former and not, vice versa. As a perception of deprivation, its applicability is clearly evident from the experience of the former socialist countries. In these 'plutocratic societies', that is, a society which is divided into a small number of rich and a large number of poor, it is the 'claim from below' that led to politico-economic transformation.

Today, India is caught in the web of globalization. As such, the concept of 'Dalit' requires a new interpretation keeping in mind the changing socio-economic configuration of the Indian society due to 'open' societies and economy. Since mid-1991, India has adopted comprehensive economic reforms, in order to integrate with the global economy through trade, investment and technology flows, for ensuring steady growth. As such, the socialist pattern of the society in India which moulded the national psyche for over four decades, suffered a major jolt. Subsequently, India is exposed to the outside socio-cultural world too, which is bound to affect the Indian society.

It is even being feared of the 'cultural implantation' of the West on the Indian society. Moreover, the recent debate on the exclusion of the 'creamy layer' from the benefits of reservation between legislature and judiciary is indicative to the fact that economic dimension has been added to the notion of 'backwardness'. On this basis, it may be argued that the Indian society is divided between 'privileged' class and 'unprivileged' class in which the former always develop a government manipulated by them. Also, without economic equality, political power will be vested in the hands of a few who are economically stronger. Therefore, political equality is never real unless it is accompanied by virtual economic equality; political power, otherwise is bound to be the handmaid of economic power. This is true in the case of the 'Dalit' leadership that after Ambedkar there is dearth of 'legitimate' leaders amongst them. Those thrown up by the community decided to turn traitorous; they got 'pocketed' by the 'privileged' class and let their community behind.

Notes

1. Fukuyama, Francis, (1989), "The End of History", *National Interest* Washington, D.C., Summer, p. 40.
2. Woods, Ngaire, (2000), *The Political Economy of Globalization,* Macmillan Press, London, p. 3.
3. Huntington, S.P., (1991), *The Third Wave: Democratization in the Twentieth Century,* University of Oklahama Press, London.
4. Rosenau, James N., (1992), "Relocation of Authority in a Shrinking World", *Comparative Politics,* New York, Vol. 24, pp. 253–72.
5. Nasbit, John, (1994), *Global Paradox,* William Morrow, New York, p. 43.
6. For detail, see Mannheim, K., (1936), *Ideology and Utopia,* London; Aron, R., (1955), *The Opium of Intellectuals*; Lipset, S.M., (1960), *Political Man,* New York.
7. Prasad, Lokesh K., (2005), "Globalization of Market Economy: Nature and Consequences" in Shailesh Choubey, et al., *Economic Reforms in India: Needs, Effects and Suggestions,* Sarup and Sons, New Delhi, p. 61.
8. Huntington, S.P., (1991), op. cit.
9. See Rosenau, James N., (1992), op. cit.
10. Brown, J.F., (1991), *Surge to Freedom: The End of Communist Rule in Eastern Europe,* The John Hopkins University Press, Durham, pp. 12–14.

11. Rosenau, James N., (1990), *Turbulence in World Politics: A Theory of Change and Continuity,* Princeton University Press, Princeton p. 381.
12. Gitelman, Z., (1990), "The Roots of Eastern Europe's Revolution", *Problems of Communism*, Washington D.C., Vol. 39, p. 89.
13. Olson, Mancur, (1990), "The Logic of Collective Action in Soviet Nationalities", *Journal of Soviet Nationalities*, London, No. 1, p. 8.
14. Johnson, Chalmers, (1991), *Revolutionary Change*, Stanford University Press, Stanford, pp. 94–104.
15. Welsh and Hancock, (1994), (eds.) *German Unification: Process and Outcomes*, Westview Press, Boulder, p. 18 j.
16. Csepili, G. and Orkay, A., (1992), "From Unjust Equality to Just Inequality", *The New Hungarian Quarterly*, Budapest, Vol. 3, p. 72.
17. Verma, Vidhu, (2006), "The State, Democracy and Global Justice", *Economic and Political Weekly*, Vol. XLI, No. 34, August 26, p. 3728.
18. Taylor, P. and Flint, C., (2000), *Political Geography: World Economy, Nation, State and Locality,* Prentice Hall, London, p. 2.
19. Prasad, Lokesh K., (2005), op. cit., pp. 14–15.
20. Strange, Susan, (1996), *The Retreat of the State: The Diffusion of Power in the World Economy,* Cambridge University Press, Cambridge, p. 51.
21. Elsehans, Hartmut, (2000), "Political Economy or Economic Politics? Prospects of Civil Society in Era of Globalization", *Indian Journal of Public Adminisration*, New Delhi, Vol. XLVI, No. 4, October-December, p. 569.
22. Frankel, Francine R., (2005), *India's Political Economy 1947–2004: The Gradual Revolution*, Oxford University Press, New Delhi, pp. 5–8.
23. See Srinivas, M.N., (1966), *Social Change in Modern India,* Los Angeles, California, Chapter 1.
24. Frankel, (2005), op. cit., p. 7.
25. Ibid., p. 8.
26. Rao, V.M., (2006), "The Elusive Goal of Empowerment: Review of the Emerging Phase in Poverty Reduction" in R. Radhakrishna, et al., *India in a Globalizing World: Some Aspects of Macro Economy, Agriculture and Poverty,* Academic Foundation, New Delhi, p. 470.
27. Basu, D.D., (1992), *Introduction to the Constitution of India*, Prentice Hall of India, New Delhi, p. 93.
28. Ibid., pp. 359–363.
29. Balaji v. State of Mysore, A.I.R., 1963, S.C. 649 (656, 658).
30. Janaki Prasad v. State of J&K, A.I.R., 1973, S.C. 930.
31. State of A.P. v. Balaram, A.I.R., 1972, S.C. 1375.
32. http://www. dalitfoundation. org/07whoaredalit/

33. *Times of India*, New Delhi, December 6, 2006.
34. The term 'higher caste' should be replaced by the word 'General Category'. Every competitive examination in India follows this pattern of social categorization.
35. *Times of India*, December 9, 2006.
36. Rao, V.M., (2006), op. cit., p. 470.
37. Ibid.
38. Comment of Vijay Tendulkar in his interview by *Times of India*, December 6, 2006.
39. Ibid.

6

Reservation for Dalits in Private Sector

BIJOY KUMAR

In recent years, essentially before and after the last general election, the idea of reservation for Dalits in the private sector has become a very controversial issue in the society. It has both supporters and opponents placing their arguments, sometimes rationally, while on some other occasions, emotionally and aggressively. Though, raised as an election stunt by the Congress-led UPA to win over a sizable votes of Dalits on its account, the issue has now assumed serious dimensions affecting some basic areas of the functioning of the society.

The literal meaning of the word *Dalit* is 'downtrodden' or 'oppressed'. This refers to those people in the society who, due to some or the other inhibitions—social, cultural, economic, political, etc.—have been deprived of the basic requirements of a dignified social life. In the Indian social context, this term generally refers to scheduled caste, scheduled tribes, backward classes and women in different social settings. These are the people who have been left far behind in the socio-economic development of the society. They have been forced to live a life of stigma, inhibitions and compulsions.

When India became independent and adopted the practices of welfare state, the theory of 'social justice' became the guiding policy of governance. The Government of India, in order to bring the Dalits in the mainstream of the society, adopted the 'Policy of Reservation and Quota' in government services. Though the policy of reservation was not enacted in its right spirit, it still remained a chief instrument of social justice because until the last decade of the previous century, the government services and the public sector units were the major areas of employment in India. Since then, a sea change has taken place in the employment sector. Under the sweeping influence of globalization, liberalization and privatization (LPG), the government has started withdrawing itself from the areas of welfare functions as well as the socio-economic development of the society, thereby shifting the responsibility of these functions into the hands of the private and corporate sector. This has resulted in a sharp decline in the potentiality of the government sector to provide jobs to its people. Hence, the private sector is being seen as a potential area where the growing workforce of India can be absorbed. And the above debate centres round the fact that which section of the society is getting what out of it.

The people who are against the idea of reservation in private sector, are apprehensive that with the application of reservation policy in this sector, merit may be compromised, thus creating again the same poor work culture and standard which have crept into the functioning of the government sector. It will be difficult to compete with the international market with such poor working force in our private industries.

Globalization has brought about de-regulation and de-control of the economic activities of the society. It is argued that, in such a situation, it will be quite difficult to implement this policy as it will be against the dominating idea of liberalization. Moreover, there is little possibility that the MNCs working in India will accept this idea. If they do not, it will not only drastically reduce job prospects in the private sector because the Indian private arena has, of late, been infested with the multinational corporations, but also create an unfavourable playing ground for the Indian private sector in the formidable international private community.

The opponents of this idea also smell some political foul play in the proposal just before the general elections. Judging by the past record of the Congress government, it has not been able to fulfil the allotted quota of reservation for the Dalits which has already been enshrined in the Constitution itself. Not only that, it failed for nearly 44 years to identify other backward classes and to begin the implementation of reservation for them. That is why, the whole exercise looks more like a political stunt and it seems that Congress wants to hide its own sins of not implementing the reservation in the government and public sector and plans to shift the onus to the private sector.

On the other hand, the protagonists of the idea of reservation for Dalits in the private sector put forward a number of strong arguments in support of the need for reservation for Dalits in the private sector, even though they already have provision for reservation in government jobs. The reservation policy in government jobs has been in operation for nearly six decades but still the share of Dalits in government jobs show a very dismal picture. In 1999, there were 481 judges in the High Courts of India out of which only 15 belonged to scheduled caste, while there were 21 judges in Supreme Court and there was not a single judge from Dalit category, in Group A Central Government Services the Dalits' participation was a meagre 10 per cent. The above scene does not seem to have changed substantially till the present day. Even in the corporate sector, the story is not very different.

It is generally argued that the above situation is due to the fact that people from the 'upper' castes are more skilled and talented. There is still a tendency to think in genetic terms, in spite of the fact that nearly all scientific studies show little 'natural' or 'biological' distinction among different social groups. In fact, it might be said that if there is genetic distinction between the 'upper' and the 'lower' castes—which would assume that there has been almost no intermingling of genes between the two groups over centuries—the advantage would be for the latter; the arduous life that the deprived sections have faced would mean that only those who are stronger and more intelligent would survive to pass on these genes. However, there is little evidence of any such separation in India. Rather, there is evidence of good deal of intermingling between social groups in spite of formal caste barriers.

What this means is that the apparent difference in 'intelligence' and 'achievement' between the 'upper' and the 'lower' castes is a result of social factors—of poverty, ill-health, lack of education and all the other factors that have served to smother the abilities and potentials of people from Dalit backgrounds. The result is that those from higher caste backgrounds with long traditions of education and intellectual activities behind them have advantages in developing their potential that the deprived masses of people do not have. The situation means that there is a vast wastage of human resources in India. It should be of greatre concern not only to Dalits themselves but to any true nationalist.

It is often argued that in an age of globalization such issues as social justice and programme for the upliftment of the Dalits no longer have any relevance. But, in a country like India, it is just the opposite which is true. A closed-in nation with little involvement and trade with the rest of the world can afford to move along slowly, to stagnate and to let the talent of its vast human population go to waste while a few take on the responsibility of 'guiding' the society. But an open nation has to stand the test of competitiveness. And the fact is that trying to compete with so much deprivation persisting in the society is like trying to engage in trade or become a world power with a population of only about two million, instead of a billion of energetic and talented people.

Unfortunately, 'social justice' and 'compensatory discrimination' programmes in India have got stereotyped around the themes of 'reservation' in the public sector. And so much of complexity has been built up around the subject that are major assumptions, which everyone takes for granted, but which are mistaken and need to be overcome. Among these, two are important: first, social justice programmes are more or less equivalent to reservation and that reservation is limited to employment in public and government sector alone. Second, which is even more debilitating is the pervasive idea that reservation is in some way at odds with 'merit' that we have to give up on or 'relax' certain standards of merit in order to do social justice for Dalits.

If reservation means compromising with merit, in that case, as we have already seen, that Dalits form only about 12 per cent of Group 'A' jobs in the public sector. And, if the government public sector is not doing well, as has been argued by some, then who are to be blamed—the 12 per cent Dalits or the 80 per cent who claim to belong to the 'meritorious' category? There is no data, scientific study or survey to establish that the Dalits are not 'good' at their work.

In fact, the main purpose of the reservation policy was to ensure social and economic justice thereby realizing the goal of the empowerment of the Dalits and tribals. It can address certain social inequalities that have pervaded Indian society for so long. Thus, the policy of job reservations intends to bring about proportional representation as it is a mode of distributing benefits based on the proportion of population. If today, the job prospects in the government sector is shinking then this benefit can very well be extended to the private sector to accommodate the growing working population in India.

What is, however, missing in this euphoria by the supporters and a lot of hue and cry by the opponents over 'private sector reservation' is the limitation of 'emancipator' role this idea can play. According to the Union Ministry of Labour (1999), the total workforce in the organized private sector was 86.98 lakh close to 9 million, which may have increased to the range of 15 million by now. As per a conservative estimate, low skilled, semi-skilled and unskilled workers add up to more than three-fourth of the workforce of the Indian private sector. Even if the idea of reservation in the private sector is put into practice, how much of the workforce it will be able to absorb? The way in which the Maharashtra government has tried to apply this idea, further limits the prospect of reservation in the private sector.

The present Indian government which is trying to sell this idea has not been able to calculate the backlog of vacancies for even primary level teaching positions in the central schools. It cannot, therefore, be expected that it will apply this principle in the right perspective.

Despite these disturbing facts, it cannot be denied that some sort of mechanism must be evolved to give proper opportunities to the Dalits in the private sector because compensatory discriminatory efforts or social justice programmes should not be limited to the public sector alone. In fact, as India is 'going global' faster than many sections of the society want it to, it is important to realize that a truly modern society requires the conscious creation of opportunities for all its citizens, and a truly competitive society cannot afford to waste any talent. This means that social justice programmes are not only in the interest of Dalits, but in the interest of the nation as a whole and they require policies that take account of every sector in a modern and growing economy. Universalizing education and health care is an essential part of this process; access to land and other property is also necessary; but so are special programmes ensuring access to employment in the private as well as public sector. If liberalization is to be successful, the private corporate cannot remain a privileged island of the 'upper' caste.

We should do away with the widespread idea that somehow 'reservation' and 'merit' are opposite to each other, and that programmes to achieve 'social justice' will slow down the development of a truly open, caste-free, merit-based society. In fact, if the Dalits too are given proper opportunity in the right perspective they can also prove to be assets for the growing Indian economy. Besides, the way job opportunities are shrinking in the public sector, some alternative areas have to be explored, otherwise, the huge growing workforce will turn out to be a liability which will wreck the whole process of socio-economic development of India.

But one must be careful that reservation in private sector should not go the way as reservation in the government jobs has turned out to be. The policy, which was initially meant for 10 years, has been in force for more than 55 years; still a sizeable population of Dalits has not been benefited from it. It has virtually created 'upper castes' within the Dalit society itself usurping all the opportunities meant for the real Dalits.

In India, it has been the tradition of governments to bring about all sorts of reform through legal sanctions without having consensus in the society on the issue. Governments feel their work over by simply passing some legislation and never think of their implementation in proper direction. That is why, the reforms have failed to bring about desired results. Here again, same story appears to have taking place. In America, private sector itself, has launched 'Affirmative Action' plan to provide due representation to Nigros, Red Indians, etc., in it, having any legal sanction behind it. In India, same procedure should be adopted. Let the private sector be responsive enough to initiate process in terms of providing due representation to Dalits in their work places and decision-making process. Because it is ultimately going to benefit it as well as the society.

At the same time, in the era of globalization, the importance of reservation as an instrument of social justice should not be exaggerated. We should remember Kanshi Ram, a veteran Dalit leader, who had once stated, "Crutches are good till you are learning to walk: they become a handicap when you want to run". Dalits too, remember that if we want to compete with the world, we cannot afford to walk. We will have to run. Here, it is not reservation but intellectualization will matter.

References

Kumar, Dr Vivek, "Reservation in Private Sector for Dalits: A Political Stunt", *Sunday Pioneer*, October 1, 2004.

Omvedt, Gail, "Reservation in the Corporate Sector", *Counter Current*, Org., May 9, 2005.

Prasad, Chandra Bhan, "Myths about Private Sector Reservation", *The Pioneer*, June 14, 2004.

Reddy, K. Vidyasagar, "Reservation in Private Sector: Not a Charity, But a Necessity", *Counter Currents*, Org., August 11, 2005.

Waghmore, Suryakant, "Reservations and Competing Nations", *Deccan Herald*, September 29, 2005.

7

Violation of Human Rights of Women and New Economic Policy

RANJANA MISHRA AND SUNIL KUMAR SHRIVASTAVA

Gender violence is universal phenomenon. Violence against women is violation of our personhood as we perceive it or dehumanize it. Violence against women carried out by any individual, group or institution or society is human rights violation.

In India, basically women are oppressed and are not treated at par with men. Her sufferings are two-fold, she has her own share of universal sufferings as a woman and additionally she is victim of a variety of exploitation—social, religious, economic and even cultural.[1]

Women working in administrative fields have to face identity crisis if they belong to Dalit—white-collared middle class—they suffer a kind of inferiority complex (about their caste and its identity). They also suffer cultural identity.[2]

In spite of this transition to their class, transformation in socio-political scenario is taking place. Last few decades have been observing change in the 'world of work' of Indian society. Although, the secular mode for the society under the Constitution all (caste, creed and gender) barriers have been written off and any Indian can offer any job. The Indian society gives an expression of openness. It is equally true for women to get equal rights in the 'world of work'.[3] However, the real change is yet to emerge.

Why women has to suffer is not a new question. Generation after generation has seen and experienced that the background (family) and environment has made her to be as she is. Socialization (political) is a process when a child becomes a full-fledged member of socio-political system. Jangam, in his book *Political Socialization*, writes that the child's membership in a particular community or class can influence his role and activities in a major way and can be regarded as a significant component of the process of 'political socialization' of the child.[4] In Hindu political system the priest class, specially the Brahmins, were advised and encouraged and expected to play a vital role of educating and enlighting people and also assisting the ruler class in conducting politics and administration. But children, because of low monetary value placed upon caring for them, that serve as one of many factors that assigns a low degree of work to women, contributing to women's low self-esteem that hinders them in attempting to participate in social-political life.[5]

While trying to understand the hurdles in the development of women, specially their participation in political life, now more concern about her socio-economic life has generally been clouded by various assumptions regarding women's behavioural pattern, their 'backward consciousness' lack of interest in public issues, or biological difference in their mental make-up, women willfully place themselves in marginal positions towards matters 'political'. The crucial problem is that women find themselves being judged and judging themselves by two standards. One standard is of their femininity, of the private world which regards them as nurturant, passive, emotional, home-oriented and subordinate to men. The other standard is that of modern role which is the standard of public world which expects women to be active, ambitious and achievement rational, oriented, competitive. It is observed (observation is also made by men) that elected women do not participate in the debate, or women elect those candidates whom their men wish to support. Subordination of women in society acts as a structural constraint to their participation in political activities. Owing to gender-based division of labour in the family, women have to bear the full responsibility of household chores. It is the women's duty to bring fuel, fodder and water to cook. They have to look after the rearing and education of children. These constraints operate almost for all classes and communities of women.[6]

But women always worked although carrying the impact of social traditions she worked not like a 'drone' in the household but an active 'bee'. Even in the primitive societies, women workers performed almost as numerous and as varied tasks as did men. In agriculture, age division of labour became fixed and was accepted as customary and proper. It was till this time women were directly in competitions with men. It was the industrial revolution[7] which brought about the change and women were assigned a tremendous change in their work pattern, where artisans were drawn into factories, women also became unskilled wage earners. Industrial capitalism brought the change and it was not the society's requirement of women work in industry, not for interest need of women but as desired by the entrepreneurs to utilize cheap labour for profit-making purposes. It is tough journey of women to work at home—home to work at factories.

Story of women in India depicts a continued way of exploitation and discrimination. The society refuses to recognize their potentialities, hard work and contribution to the welfare of the society. Specially, they are still considered to be unequal, and inferior to men.[8] They are called 'fair sex' and are shown 'unfair treatment'.

Although, Dalit woman who fortunately had not fallen prey into the net cunningly woven by Hinduism was more free and less dependent. She was physically strong and could work hard. The problems of *sati*, widowhood, child marriage, female infanticide were considered as social stigma[9] in so-called educated society, were not found in Dalits, divorce and remarriage were not restricted in their society. But slowly, the freedom was mercilessly taken away. They were forced into subjugation, widowhood, no trust upon them. Today, Dalit women constitute a major working force, are thrice alienated and oppressed on the basis of their caste, class or gender.[10]

Dalit women are found to be less educated and in low-paid jobs. Dalit women work under the most exploitative, dehumanizing and unhealthy conditions, neither their work, nor wages are regularized. They are denied all basic amenities (even drinking water), proper health care and constantly have been facing the insecurity of being evicted from their places where they manage their lives and livelihood. An analysis of 40 rape victims revealed that more than 80 per cent of them belonged to the lower caste, Dalit and tribal groups and also from the poor classes of society.[11]

Unfortunately, their class of society rarely focussed as speaking in their own voices and coping with their own lives and difficulties. Their lives were never studied except statistical analysis of work participation were done. On the whole, they echoed the issues such as state violence, denial of land rights, social and legal discrimination, infringement of civil liberties, inferior status, dehumanizing living and working conditions.[12] Their status of illiteracy and ignorance, social ostracism and untouchabilities maintained by the caste Hindus as well as other religions are of a serious nature in terms of violation of human rights in India.[13]

Human rights of a woman is the "collection rights of a woman to be seen and accepted as a person with the capacity to decide or act on her own behalf and to have equal access to resources and equitable social, economic and political support to develop her full potential, exercise her right as a full woman being and to support the development of other".[14] It is seen and observed that violation of human rights of women in many fields have become a general practice. It is necessary to observe this view in context with new economic policy and reforms made or expected to be made there after.

India has adopted a clear policy for protection of human rights for its citizens. Right to equality prohibits any discrimination on grounds of religion, caste, sex or place of birth, etc.

Equality of opportunity is related to employment abolition of untouchability.

Right to freedom assures all citizens freedom of speech, association, travel, residence, etc.,[15] and also acquisition of property and practise any occupation.

Rights against exploitation prohibits forced labour and child labour.

There have been various unconventions relating specially to human rights of women. Indian Constitution also assures 'equal pay for equal work'.[16] Let us ask ourselves, is it all working as they are expected to? Are these assurances even by the constitution truly working with its soul?

An analysis of problems of women working in the unorganized sector throws light on the sexist attitude of mainstream of trade unions. It is well known that women constitute a majority of the unorganized labour force. The working condition in this sector is abyssemal. There is no job security, no fair wages, no facility and no rights to demand for improvement of their situation. Although some organizations like WWF and SEWA ventilate their problems.[17]

In spite of best efforts the voices raised by women organizations are shut down, harassment at workplace continued. They are threatened for arrest or rape. All such measures are taken to demoralize a woman. Even after the expected change due to the 73rd constitutional amendment, women do came forward for participating in democracy. But, the real picture revealed a different story. "The multiplicity of functions and responsibilities placed upon ill-equipped and ill-trained staff in public offices and local institutions make it almost impossible to deliver services with any degree of efficiency particularly in rural areas: For example, a 'multipurpose' female health worker is required to perform as many as 47 tasks to be undertaken on a regular basis."[18]

In industrial sector, women are assigned with those occupations which did not call for particular skill or those for which they showed special aptitude. Certain jobs were named as 'women's jobs'.[19]

There have been welfare measures taken by the Government of India (Ministry of Human Resource Development and also Ministry for Family and Health Welfare). In 1985 Women and Child Development Department established four bureaus for:

1. Child development.
2. Child welfare.
3. Development of women.
4. Bureau for the welfare of woman.

This department has four organizations working under it:

1. Rashtriya Jan Sahayog aur Baal Vikas Sansthan.
2. Rashtriya Mahila Kosh.
3. Kendriya Samaj Kalyan Board.
4. Rashtriya Mahila Aayog (Working for the protection of rights of women, established in 1992).

Other organizations and services are Kalyan Sahayata Sewa, Rozgaar aur Prashishkshan, Samajik aur Sarthik Karyakram, and then Swayam Siddha Yojna, Indira Vikas Yojna (both working as programme for women's rights). Swarshakti Pariyojna to encourage women to form social work organizations, to promote and encourage to work for better standards of life.

In 2001–02, Swadhar Yojna was started to help poor and helpless women, women suffering after natural calamities, to advise them, guide them for hygiene and health matters, to develop some kind of skill. In 1997, a programme against exploitation of women was started to look after prostitutes and their children.[20]

Human Rights Development Report (1998) has suggested following for the development of women:

1. Nutritious food.
2. Education.
3. Availability of potable water.
4. Improved health and sanitation facilities.[21]

But it is sad to see the development of women is far behind. On a broaden plane it could be said that there has been much discrimination against women all over India. A much more bold step towards her upliftment is yet to be adopted and implemented seriously. Education, training, information and above all economic security and legal literacy are some essential requirements. "We need well-defined division of responsibility and accountability", "We need fiscal empowerment", "We need freedom of information and full disclosure of financial decisions made by government".[22]

We need a sustainable conscious and deliberate effort, if we really want to change the status and condition of women, without being hypocratic.

Notes

1. Fatima Siddhiqui and Sarla Raughathan, *Women and Human Rights* Part I, Kanishka Publishers, p. 377.
2. M.N., Sivprakasan, *Dalit and Social Mobilization,* Rajat Publication, pp. 147–48.
3. Prabhakar Rani, *Third World Sociology*, Dominant Publishers and Distributors, Vol. II, p. 75.
4. Maya Majumdar, *Protecting Our Women*, Dominant Publishers, pp. 1–2.
5. Fatima Siddhiqui, *Women and Human Rights,* p. 377.
6. Maya Majumdar, *Protecting Our Women,* Vol. I, Dominant Publishers, pp. 50–52.
7. P.M. Parmar, *Social Work and Social Welfare in India,* Sublime Publications, p. 70.

8. P.M. Parmar, *Social Work and Social Welfare in India*, Sublime Publications, p. 130.
9. S.K. Chahal, *Dalits Patronized*, Shubhi Publications, p. 230.
10. P.M. Parmar, *Social Work and Social Welfare in India*, Sublime Publications, p. 131.
11. M.N. Sivprakasan, *Dalits and Social Mobilization*, Rajat Publications, p. 133.
12. S.K. Chahal, *Dalits Patronized*, Shubhi Publication, p. 233.
13. Fatima, Siddhiqui and Sarla, Ranganathan, *Women and Human Rights*, Part I, Kanishka Publishers, p. 377.
14. Maya Majumdar, *Protecting Our Women*, Dominant Publishers, p. 334.
15. D.D. Basil, The Constitution of India.
16. Article 39 (D).
17. C.M. Choudhary and Arvind Jain, *Labour Legislation in India*, Indus Valley Publications.
18. Part of Article of Bimal Jalan, www.hi.org.in/scripts.
19. P.M. Parmar, *Social Work and Social Welfare in India*, Sublime Publishers, pp. 71–72.
20. *India, 2003*, Publication Department, Ministry of Telecommunication, pp. 289–295.
21. M.N. Sivprakasan, *Dalits and Social Mobilization*, Rajat Publications, p. 338.
22. Online Article by Bimal Jalan on "India's Economy in the Twenty First Century: A New Beginning or a False Dawn?" www.rbi.org.in (Date of Publication—February 8, 2001).

8

Indian Ethos of Globalization

MAHAVIR PRASAD MODI

There cannot be life without change, and the pace of change in human life is faster in our time than ever before. In previous centuries, we had a limited vision of the world. Today, a new world society is gradually emerging. The term 'globalization' is not easy to define. It is a new buzzword that has come to dominate the world since 1990s. For some people, globalization is a dirty word. It conveys the nation that rich multinational corporations are now sweeping through and dominating the whole world in a new form of imperialism. Anti-globalizers point to data that show that poverty has decreased very slowly, if at all, in the last decade since the collapse of the Soviet Union. The present generation of the human race has a lesson to learn from the Indian tradition.

Poverty

No doubt, mass poverty is a challenge to the global community. According to the World Bank in 1998, 1.2 billion people lived in absolute poverty, i.e., with an income of less than one dollar a day. Although poverty has decreased, it remains the biggest challenge to mankind. Poverty has a de-humanizing effect. It keeps people from realizing their inherent human potential, forces them into unequal relationships that severely limit their freedom, exposes them almost defencelessly to the predatory behaviour of others. The daily struggle for survival usually does not leave the poor, time to participate in the political life of their community or nation, except in the service of a patron. Poverty is, therefore, a huge challenge for liberals, both for their vision of humanity and their vision of a just liberal society. Liberals believe in the principle of freedom of the individual and a set of an alienable human rights. Extreme poverty is a daily attack on the right to life of an individual and therefore cannot be tolerated by liberals. Moreover, a person struggling for physical survival has very few choices in life where he or she could experience individual freedom. A realization of individual liberty throughout society presupposes an alleviation of mass poverty. Poor people usually have no choice but to sell their political rights to a patron who provides them with a modicum of security, a situation that seriously threatens democracy. Societies managed to transform themselves into real democracies only when poverty was reduced and such patron-client-relationships became less dominant.

Gillin defines poverty as "that condition in which a person, either because of inadequate income or unwise expenditures, does not maintain a scale of living high enough to provide for his physical and mental efficiency and to enable him and his natural dependents to function usefully according to the standards of the society of which he is a member".[1] Every society describes certain standards of living regarding minimum food, clothing, shelter, education and other amenities. Those who fall below this culturally prescribed standard, popularly known as poverty line, are classified as poor.[2] Poverty caused by ignorance, unfair and unjustifiable exploitation as well as natural disaster. It is a sociological concept, it reduces one from a human being with dignity to a sub-human and it exists in every country of the world. Poverty has physical effect on the person, such as family problems, poor nutrition, poor health, illiteracy, shabby appearance and lack of shelter and clothing.

Poverty has grown and spread to such an extent that it now threatens social and political stability and is a serious block to the attainment of sustainable development. Fortunately, with the worldwide recognition of the exient and depth of the problem, have come the knowledge, skill and capital to eradicate this light of human insensitivity. There is mounting evidence that the general breakdown of human security and hopes for the future have much to do with poverty and injustice.

South Asian countries account for almost a quarter of the world's population. These countries are Bangladesh, Bhutan, Maldives, Nepal, Pakistan, Sri Lanka and India. Despite more than four decades of development in South Asia, the number of poor has risen and continues to rise. The resulting burden is too large for society to carry. Poverty in this region in the year 1991, based on the conventional 'poverty line' estimates in most countries, would be between 330 to 440 million. The magnitude and complexity of the problem of poverty in South Asia is staggering. Around 30 to 40 per cent of the population of South Asia is living below the poverty line.

Globalization

The last quarter of the 20th century has witnessed an upsurge of the process of globalization. After 1990, the world is rapidly changing due to global structure of the production, trade and communication. The world is becoming one through the revolution in telecommunication, transportation and formation of global financial market. Today, financial market constitute a fully global economy. Originally, the expression 'globalization' had its faint beginnings in the 1960s in the writings of French and American scholars. Steadily, it has gained currency as a "kind of lived experience of our generation". In its contemporary usage, the concept of globalization has come to reflect "a widespread perception that the world is being rapidly moulded into a shared social space by economic and technological forces and that development for the one region of the world can have profound consequences for the life chances of individual or communities on the other side of the globe".

Globalization is not a simple, but a complex set of process that operates at multiple levels of politics, economics, culture and ideology. It is a social process in which the constraints of geography on social and cultural arrangements recede and this is actually happening.

The word 'globalization' is used in many senses. First, globalization entails that events, decisions and activities in one part of the world have almost immediate significance for individuals and communities in other parts of the globe. Secondly, global processes are increasingly autonomous since they occur independently of the authorities and institutions of the nation-state.[3] Some of the analysts emphasize that globalization is a new historical process. The processes with worldwide reach are not of a recent origin yet the ongoing globalization process and discussions about it contain new and distinctive elements. The current process of globalization coincides with the liberalization of international capital, movements in the early 1970s. The development of information technology and computerization are also mentioned as key factors of the ongoing globalization process. The neo-liberals claim that the process brings free and universal benefits, whereas anti-neo-liberals equate it with social and environmental destruction.

Although a precise definition of 'globalization' is still unavailable, it has already become a cliche of our times. There is no cogent theory of globalization, nor even a systematic analysis of its major features. Briefly stated, the hyperglobalizationists view globalization as a new era in which people everywhere are increasingly subjected to the unavoidable disciplines of the global market place. There is a shared conviction that economic globalization is constructing new forms of social organization that are supplanting, or that will eventually supplant, traditional nation-states as the primary economic and political units of world society.

Economic globalization is a reality of contemporary life. The term 'globalization' signifies a market-driven economy in which finance capital, floating seemingly unhindered across national frontiers, currencies and continents, occupies a preponderant position over productive as well as local or national-based capital. Globalization is a qualitative and not a quantitative term. The phenomenon it denotes represents a new stage of high-tech capitalism which manifests itself as another variant of imperialism.[4]

Briefly, globalization is irreversible. How to make it compatible with our culture, polity and economy is the real question? While the necessity of achieving fast economic growth and modern technology cannot be denied, the questions relating to poverty, regional and social inequalities, unemployment, empowerment of the weaker and unprivileged sections of Indian society cannot easily be brushed aside. All such questions are directly connected with our political stability. Hence, we have to look for a globalization that includes rather than marginalizes the poor. We need to evolve a strong and responsive system of governance.[5]

Globalization has generated widespread social, economic and cultural insecurity. It is not the cross-cultural interaction of diverse societies but an imposition of a particular culture on all others. It is the predation of one class, one race, one nation and often one gender. In 'global' the dominant 'local' seeks global control. The global is not universal human interest, it represents a particular interest and culture which has been globalized through its reach and control.[6]

Indian Ethos of Globalization

The Indian missionaries of an Indian philosophy, Buddhism, were the first people in history to think and feel in terms of the human race. They felt a concern for all their fellow human beings, they had a vision of mankind as being potentially a single family and they set themselves to turn this potential unity into an accomplished fact by peaceful persuasion. Taking clue from the diverse paradigms of globalization and liberalization that have prevailed in the different countries of the world economy, the question arises as to what should be the genuinely indigenous Indian paradigm of globalization. It is essential that we identify our own model of globalization which would be an integral part of the social and cultural ethos of the Indian economic society. Mahatma Gandhi gave India a genuinely Indian style of revolution. The intellectuals, businessmen and the policy makers should evolve a truly indigenous approach to the task of the economic governance to suit our national interest of optimal welfare. In the context of India in the world economy, he had expressed the views that we should keep our doors and windows open, but we should not allow our feet to be swept away by the blowing wind. All initiatives of development and structural changes should be from the view point of their implications for the poorest of the poor in the country.

While speaking about the Indian ethos of governance, one feels tempted to digress a bit on the Indian ethos based upon our classical wisdom, which was in fact the basis for Gandhian thoughts. The Indian classical thoughts of governance provide a harmonious blend of globalization and national interests. There are many contrasting features between the modern conception of globalization and liberalization and the thoughts embedded in the Indian classical thoughts. There is need for some fundamental thinking on the scope and meanings of market-driven globalization in the context of achieving optimum human welfare. The basic principle of globalization in the classical thoughts is one of placing global welfare as the prime mover for individual action. As against this, the modern way of globalization places global action in the forefront in achieving individual benefits.

The Upanishadic statement that the entire world is like a family and that all the resources of the universe belong to the society (God) and each individual has only that share which legitimately belongs to him brings out the global concerns contained in the Indian classical thoughts.

Swadeshi

Swadeshi is the key concept in Gandhi's philosophy. It is not merely an economic doctrine but also has ideological implications. In Swadeshi, Gandhi found an answer to psychological and political problems of the country. Gandhi says, "My nationalism is as broad as my Swadeshi. I want India's rise so that the whole world may benefit. I do not want India to rise on the ruin of other nations".[7] He says further, "No nation on earth has risen without adopting Swadeshi as the principle of life".[8]

Swadeshi is people-centred and not government-centred. It refers to self-reliance and self-control ranging from individual to society. Gandhi was concerned with the value and dignity of every man. Gandhi's respect for the individual arises from his faith in God. God is impartial and selfless. So, by following the path of God we follow the path of truth and non-violence. Empowering individual opens the way to socio-economic justice.[9]

Swadeshi is not obsolete in today's context. It is the creative alternative to the rule of centralized nation-state as well as the rule of global corporations and institutions such as WTO. Swadeshi as conceived by Gandhi was not against either internationalism or universal brotherhood. According to him, the main aim of Swadeshi was the protection of the home industry. Gandhi did not favour isolation of India from the world. He categorically asserted that his Swadeshi provided for foreign import if it was useful for the country or the people.

Today, Swadeshi is not a reactionary idea. It is an important concept of strengthening Indian industry and creating India multi-nationalist. Swadeshi means trusting our own genius to handle our own problems that are unique to ourselves. In fact, no country has risen to heights without paying proper attention to its indigenous institutions and resources. It does not mean that we isolate ourselves from the world or that the process of liberalization should be reversed. We should put more emphasis on social policies, education, poverty and raising standards of living of our people. We have to place greater emphasis on labour intensive sector than on capital and technology.

Voluntary restraint on self-consumption and voluntary sharing of surplus with others characterize the classical thoughts. As against this, maximization of consumption as a modality for maximum welfare and unlimited urge or protecting and preserving the surplus with the individuals, characterize the modern ethos of economic governance. While cooperation and partnership in sharing knowledge, technology, manpower and resources characterize the classical paradigm, competition even to the extent of being predative—and protection of intellectual property characterize the modern ethos. While the Indian classical ethos gives emphasis on the duty-conscious human resource, the modern market-driven ethos gives emphasis to the rights-conscious human resource. Commissions on human rights are set up in the recent days, but there are no commissions on human duties. While the emphasis in market-driven, paradigm is on preservation of self-interest by individual entities, the emphasis in the classical ethos is on more profound concept of self-realization, meaning thereby that each individual should engage himself in performing his duties for maximum satisfaction of his conscience or inner-self.

India possesses the clout of a large potential market for investment and trade. India has the clout of very large technical and scientific manpower. However, India lacks in a disciplined and motivated manpower and more than anything else the status of India has been bogged down in all international fields with the mage of a weak and non-assertive state. India's image as a weak state continues to act as a constraint to its abilities to choose the right kind of globalization, liberalization and privatization strategies which suit its national interests in the best possible manner.

The basic issues of economic governance should be understood and analyzed in a fundamental framework which is relevant to the Indian society which considers man in a holistic framework and not just as an economic man engaged in maximization of material benefits, which is the conception in the current day economic science.

What Should India Do?

1. India should adopt the approach of selectivity in regard to globalization.
2. Foreign direct investment should be permitted and encouraged only in those sectors which would significantly contribute to income generation, employment creation and not for export earnings.
3. The approach of globalizing the financial markets without commensurate globalization of the real sector, could have dangerous consequences.
4. India should endeavour to strengthen the infrastructure and human resources covering areas such as universal literacy and health for all, for improving what one may call as the social capability of the economy for taking advantages of the globally competitive environment.
5. It is necessary that the industrial organizations structure should be based upon the principles of blending competition and cooperation on the lines of industrial clusters and cooperative societies, for facilitating optimum utilization of the scarce resources of knowledge and information.
6. India should take leadership role on various international economic issues for mobilizing support from like-minded countries of the world.
7. Liberalization should necessarily means de-bureaucratisation of the decision-making process in the economy. This kind of liberalization would require significant effort to reform and remotivate the bureaucracy, both at the level of the central government and at the state governments. India's image in the global scene would be very poor unless the bureaucratic procedures are streamlined and the delay of bureaucratic sanctions and permits are considerably reduced.
8. India is the best suited to continue to be in the framework of mixed economy, in which the public sector, private sector and the cooperative sector coexist, as also in which the state planning and the market function in a framework of mutual harmony and concordance.

9. The final point which needs to be made with all emphasis at our command is that India should not give up its aspirations for maintaining and strengthening the paradigm of intellectual self-reliance for taking its own decisions to serve its national interest.

Notes

1. Gillin, J.K. and others, *Social Problems*, Bombay, 1965, p. 388.
2. Punit, A.E., *Profile of Poverty in India*, B.R. Publishing Corporation, Delhi, 1982, p. 33.
3. Allrdt, Erik, Globalization and Prospect for Democracy and the Welfare State. Public lecture delivered at World Institute for Development, Economics Research on March 25,1999.
4. The *I.J.P.S.*, Vol. 62, No. 3, p. 376.
5. *Social Sciences Research Journal*, Vol. 8, Nos. 1 and 2, p. 130.
6. Shiva, Vandana, "Arthic Swaraj of Economic Slavery?", *The Observer,* February 3, 1998.
7. Gandhi, M.K., *An Autobiography: The Story of My Experiments with Truth,* Navjivan Publishing House, Ahmedabad, 1940.
8. *Collected Works of Mahatma Gandhi*, Publication Division, Government of India, New Delhi, 1958, Vol. XV, p. 379.
9. For details see, G.S. Herbert, "Ghandhiji on Poverty", *Sarvodaya*, Vol. XXII, February, 1973.

9

Globalization and Poverty Alleviation

BIDYA S. BIBHUTI

Globalization can be defined as a process that increases the opportunities for interaction between people all around the globe. This interaction can be economic as well as social, political, scientific or otherwise. While this article focuses on the economic aspects of globalization, it is important to keep in mind that many other dimensions are involved.

The process of economic globalization is powered by the declining costs of long distance travel, transport and communication, as well as it is the growing institutional and legal framework for international interaction between citizens and companies. Some of it is due to technological progress such as the spread of information technology. Some of it is due to international institution-building such as the trade liberalization negotiations under the General Agreement on Tariffs and Trade (GATT) that led to the establishment of the World Trade Organization (WTO). A lot is due to the individual liberalization steps that most countries have undertaken during the last decades to integrate their economies into the world market.

The result has been a spectacular increase in the volume of international trade and cross-border investment worldwide. World trade almost doubled between 1977 and 1987, and the ratio of trade to GDP (in purchasing parity $) rose from 20.6 to 29.6 per cent during this period (World Bank, World Development Indicators,

1999). This indicates the substantial rise in international exchange, i.e., how much trade is involved in producing the global sum-total of goods and services produced.

Foreign direct investment totalled 400 billion $ in 1977, seven times more in real terms than in the 1970s. The daily turnover in foreign exchange markets has increased from 10–20 billion $ in the 1970s to 1.5 trillion $ in 1997. International bank lending grew from 265 billion $ in 1975 to 4.2 million $ in 1994. Around 140 million people live and work abroad today, compared to 84 million in 1975.

As a whole, the world is much better off, per capita income has tripled in the last 50 years, the share of people enjoying medium human development has risen from 55 per cent to 66 per cent during the period 1975 to 1977, whereas the percentage of people living in low human development has fallen from 20 per cent to 10 per cent (UNDP, Human Development Report, 1999).

Globalization increases the gains from specialization, companies can source their inputs from new sources which tends to bring down costs and to improve quality. They also get access to the latest technology at lower prices, which raises productivity. They can find new markets for their products, increasing their profitability. Consumers benefit from the increased competition between produces, offering a much wider selection of goods and services, which usually translates into lower costs and better quality and hence, a higher standard of living.

A globalized capital market gives capital-starved countries access to a larger pool of capital that provided by domestic saving, thus lowering interest rates and increasing investment. More investment, more productivity and lower prices all contribute to faster GDP growth.

Firstly, the benefits of globalization are realized through increased competition. While competition lies at the heart of a successful market economy, it is heartily disliked by all the participants, especially on the producer side. In many instances, there are inefficient producers who have grown not due to their competitiveness, but due to protection or some other form of patronage. Their survival is threatened by the withdrawal of these privileges, and they will obviously fight this tooth and nail.

Another perceived drawback of globalization is that it implies a certain loss of sovereignty as certain parameters of economic policy making are governed by international agreements and are thus removed from further democratic discussion.

Globalization benefits first those who produced goods or services competitively that can be internationally traded. Therefore there are fears, that globalization will not benefit the poor and they might be displaced by international competition.

This line of reasoning, however underestimates the capacity of the poor to participate in international trade. Many sectors that will benefit from international integration offer employment opportunities for the poor, such as export oriented agriculture, small-scale industries or transport services. More seriously, it omits the benefits of lower prices and better quality of consumer goods that benefit the poor directly.

The Indian Scenario

So far, India has followed an inward looking policy. The socialism espoused by Nehru concentrated on building up domestic industries, with a large role assigned to state-owned enterprises. Although private ownership of industry was allowed, competition was curtailed by a licensing permit raj.

This economic system was supposed to bring faster industrialization than a free market economy and hence to reduce poverty faster. Judging by its own objectives, it has failed to do so. Mass poverty in India has declined much slower than in other Asian developing countries that have adopted more market-friendly outward looking policy. It is therefore difficult to see why the status quo should be preferred over increased participation in globalization, as the status quo is highly unsatisfactory for the poor.

India's economic reforms since 1991, have focussed on India's links with the world markets. India has devalued the exchange rate, abolished the licensing system for industry, reduced trade protectionism and liberalized foreign investment. Less has happened on the domestic side. The system of controls and subsidies in agriculture is still largely in place, privatization of the huge public sector has started at slow rate, which means that few funds have been freed for investment in social and physical infrastructure. The problematic labour laws have not been touched at all.

How could globalization benefit the poor? Integration in world market allows the economy to reach a higher growth rate of GDP and India's experience has shown that the post-liberalization phase has indeed led to a higher growth rate. This will bring poverty down, although to what extent depends on the internal structure of the economy. It is true that economic growth is not the only instrument needed for poverty alleviation. Investment in education and health are important as well.

The poor in India do have something to offer to the world market. Already, around 30 per cent of India's exports are generated by small-scale industry which offers employment opportunities to the poor and the potential is much higher, given the institutional and infrastructural bottlenecks that hit this sector especially hard.

The growth of new export industries such as the software industry that globalization has induced might not benefit the poor directly, as they do not have the skills needed, but these new industries in turn create demand for goods and services that give employment opportunities to the poor. There is no empirical evidence that this has displaced Indian companies to any significant degree, hence most of this additional investment has created additional employment opportunities, although here again the skilled workers would have benefited more.

What is important to keep in mind is that the poor are better off than before due to additional employment opportunities. The middle class skilled workers gains are just relatively bigger. Hence inequality of income increases, a result of globalization that the opponent of globalization nevertire of pointing out. But, it is safe to assume that the poor care more about whether their income increases or not than about statistical measurements of income inequalities. Another point that should not be ignored is the demonstration effect. Since skilled workers benefit more from the new opportunities, the incentives to invest in the education of children increases.

Since most of the poor still live in the rural areas, their fate is linked to that of agriculture. The Nehruvian system has transferred resources from agriculture to industry, thus harming the rural poor. An overvalued exchange rate and high tariff protection has increased the price of manufactured goods far above world market levels, whereas prices for many agricultural products were controlled to keep them below world market levels. Even when one of the factors in the subsidies given for power, water and fertilizer, Indian agriculture still faced with a substantial negative subsidy.

The devaluation of the exchange rate, the lowering of tariff and the increased competition faced by domestic industries has improved the terms of trade for agriculture, but the negative subsidy still remains. Further integration into the world market would therefore offer substantial benefits to the agricultural sector and hence to the poor.

On a more general level, the poor will benefit from the lower prices for goods and services that globalization will bring through increased competitions. This benefit to everybody far outweighs the losses suffered by those who are employed in uncompetitive firms and might lose their jobs. This lowering of prices raises the purchasing power of the poor as the same budget will allow them to purchase more goods and services. This increases domestic demand, in turn stimulating domestic industry.

The migration of labour is another form in which globalization can benefit the poor. New employment opportunities have arisen even for unskilled workers. Their remittances and the goods that they import form another link with the world markets and the government has been forced to relax certain controls on the movement of capital and goods due to this phenomenon. India is now the biggest recipient of remittances.

The increased competition that globalization induces undoubtedly leads to adjustment pains and some of these costs are borne by a segment of the poor—those employed in uncompetitive activities such as part of the cottage industry sector. It has been the story of the human race in the last two centuries that technological progress has rendered countless professions obsolete, and this has caused real pains. But, the answer cannot be to try to stop the process. That would be unrealistic. Investment in infrastructure to improve the links of rural areas with metropolitan and global market may be another crucial need in this direction.

Globalization does not mean that the state should abdicate its responsibilities. Indeed, the point to note is that under Nehruvian socialism, India's performance in these sectors has not been satisfactory. So, reform is needed here too. Globalization vs social spending is a false contradiction. Redirecting government expenditure from a bloated public sector to a starved social sector, using better instruments, including market-based ones, is the real challenge. This will help to realize the full benefits of globalization for the poor.

10

Impact of Economic Reforms on Dalits

SANJEEV KUMAR SINHA

The period of over 14 years, since the acceleration of the process of economic liberalization in June 1991 by the then Congress government, which did not have a parliamentary majority, has seen an orchestrated attempt by successive governments, international agencies such as the World Bank and the International Monetary Fund, official economists to portray the policies of liberalization, privatization and globalization (LPG) as both inevitable and desirable. The neo-liberal reform programme which C.P. Chandrashekhar and Jayati Ghosh point out, "made curtailment of the fiscal deficit the fundamental task of fiscal policy. It accelerated trade liberalization, which involved doing away with quantitative restrictions on imports and reducing customs tariffs, with attendant revenue implications. It dismantled control on free operations of large industrial capital, domestic and foreign. It provided a host of direct and indirect concessions to industry, reducing the tax base of the government further. It provided a host of concessions to foreign investors in the hope that they would use India as a base for world market production".[1]

The neo-liberal reformers had argued that economic growth in India was being stifled by the intrusive role of the state as both regulator and participant; that large fiscal deficits crowded out private investment and undermined investor confidence. They argued that the excessive protection provided to Indian industry by the imposition of import restrictions and tariffs prevented the development of an efficient, competitive economy which would enable India to benefit from integration with the world capitalist economy. Their claim, then, was that liberalization would enhance the growth rate. As growth occurred across the board, and the economy became more competitive through domestic deregulation and external opening-up, exports would surge and employment would expand rapidly. As a result, poverty would decline sharply as would unemployment. Economic reforms essentially means the adoption of 'Washington Consensus'. According to Guy Standing, Director of the ILO's Socio-Economic Security Programme, "Washington Consensus means a policy of economic liberalization, relying much more on markets; a reduced role for the state and. more important, for organizations and institutions; the liberalization of social policy; and in recent years the privatization of pension and health schemes and so on".[2] "Under the influence of these Bretton Woods institutions sponsored reforms, inequality in the world has been consistently growing. Between 1988 and 1993, the per capita income of the low income countries of the world fell by 35 per cent from $584 to $380. As against this, the same for the rich countries went from $17,080 to $23,090."[3]

Status of Dalits in India

In the social stratification of the traditional Hindu society, *Shudras* stood at the bottom of the ladder and were meted out the most inhuman treatment of untouchability. "Dalits are kept at the bottom of the social ladder, as 'outcastes' and 'untouchables' outside the four-tier structure."[4] The scheme of the Constitution envisaged, the report says, a three-pronged strategy for changing the status of Dalits, classified as being among the scheduled castes and the scheduled tribes, based on the traditional social order. The strategy was meant to remove the disabilities and other constraints suffered by Dalits, provide for punitive action against violence inflicted on them, and protect their economic interests through legal and legislative measures. Despite the abolition of this inhuman practice of untouchability by Article 17 of the Constitution of India, the scars of the age old exploitation of this extremely unfortunate social group still persist in the form of continuing socio-economic backwardness of these people. The term 'Dalits' is used to signify these ex-untouchables of India. Obviously, most of the Dalits are still the poorest of the poor. They happen to be the poorest and the most vulnerable section of Indian society. This is the group of society that has taken the worst beating in the last 18 years of economic change in India.

Dalits as Workforce

Today, Dalits (SCs/STs) constitute 24.56 per cent of India's total population, of which 37.98 per cent are in the category of main workers. Main workers, as defined by the census, are "those who work six months, or more than that in a year". The main workforce reflects the overall socio-economic condition of the entire population. As per the census report of 1991, of the total Dalit main workforce, 77 per cent SCs and 90.02 per cent STs are still tied to the most oppressive primary sector (agriculture and allied) of Indian economy. Further, of the total Dalit main workforce in this sector, 63.72 per cent SCs and 36.31 per cent STs are landless agricultural labour. More than 75 per cent of the Dalit workers are still connected with land; 25 per cent being the marginal and small farmers and balance over 50 per cent are the landless labourers. In urban areas, they work mainly in unorganized sector. Out of the total Dalit population of 138 million, the number of Dalits in services falling in the domain of reservations does not exceed 1.1 million; a mere 0.8 per cent.

Dalit Landholdings

The agricultural census of India (1985–86) shows that of the total Datit landholdings, 86.6 per cent SCs and 64.8 per cent STs fall in the marginal and small categories. This means that an overwhelming majority of the Dalit population in agrarian India does not have its own sources of sustenance and depends on landowners' land for their sustenance. In short, nearly 90 per cent of the Dalit population is leading a life of misery, hunger, malnutrition, ill-health, illiteracy and indignity even after 53 years of independence. "In fact, sincere and strict implementation of laws relating to land reforms, particularly the land ceiling law, which aims to distribute surplus land to the landless, would have greatly enhanced the socio-economic conditions of Dalits who constitute a substantial proportion of the agricultural labour."[5]

The major portion of government's grants, including subsidies to agricultural inputs, credit facilities, high-yielding seeds, agricultural implements, irrigation and power facilities, and infrastructural facilities (including facilities for storage and cold storage) are cornered by landlords and rich peasants who are the politically influential sections in the bourgeois-landlord political parties in rural India. In areas where the Left and progressive movements are weak, these sections control cooperatives and PRIs. The richer sections make use of these institutions for their narrow benefit and against the interest of the overwhelming majority of the peasantry. Liberalization policies, based on the retreat of the state and surrender to the capitalist market, have aggravated the crisis in agriculture further. The liberalization process is based in favour of the rich and against the interests of the poor, who are mainly agricultural labourers, poor peasants and middle peasants.

Impact of New Economic Policy on Dalit Agricultural Labourers

The second phase of capitalist development during liberalization period witnessed a reactionary change in the policies of the state. Many steps have been taken by the state to withdraw from economic affairs and to hand over everything to capitalist market forces to decide. The poor have suffered most during the period of liberalization. In the place of state-sponsored capitalist development, a strategy of development based on trade came into existence. Most non-Left state governments are taking steps to reverse the land reform process by relaxing land-ceiling and tenancy laws in order to develop the land market. The Government of Karnataka has amended the Land Reform Act of 1961 reintroducing land leasing, allowing both agriculturists and industrialists to own land and removing land ceiling for aquaculture, horticulture, floriculture and the housing industry. The Government of Maharashtra has relaxed restrictions on the conversion of agricultural land to non-agricultural land. The Agriculture Land Ceiling Act has been amended to permit large land holdings. Many non-Left governments have given thousands of hectares of land either on sale or on lease at throw away prices to multinational companies and domestic monopolies. Wasteland has been given to multinational companies and big business for development and cultivation. Instead of vesting forest land to the Adivasis who cultivate it, the central government has issued a circular calling for the forcible eviction of lakhs of adivasis from the land. Many non-Left state governments have begun the process of eviction; the Left Front state governments of Tripura and West Bengal have, however, refused to implement such a measure.

As a result of policies of liberalization, there have been drastic cuts in public investment in areas such as irrigation, electricity, science and technology, and infrastructural facilities. Public sector investment played a crucial role in the development of irrigation, power, agricultural research, roads, markets and communications. As a result of current policies of liberalization, investment declined from 1.6 per cent of the GDP in 1993–94 to 1.3 per cent of the GDP in 1998–99. This decline was mainly due to the fall in public investment. The share of agriculture and allied sectors in total gross capital formation (GCF) also declined during the period of liberalization. Contrary to what was claimed at the time of initiating this process, liberalization policies have been responsible for the decline in investment.

The share of agriculture to the GDP has declined from 61 per cent in 1950–51 to 24.2 per cent in 2001–02. But the population dependent on agriculture has declined marginally from 77 per cent to 69 per cent during this period.

The persistent decline in the relative productivity and income of agricultural worker is a serious disturbing trend. Productivity per worker in non-agricultural activity was 1.8 times that of an agricultural worker in 1950; it had risen to 4.3 times that of an agricultural worker in 1997. Workforce diversification is also not taking place in India.

One of the other disturbing features of current development is the very low employment generating potential of growth in the tertiary sector, which was the fastest growing sector during this period. In the earlier period, agriculture was a fast growing sector but it had a very high employment potential. The result is the increasing concentration of workforce in agriculture and continuous decline of relative productivity, income and living conditions of workers engaged in agriculture.

Agricultural workers and poor peasants are the worst sufferers of the policies of the government. A large proportion of them come from Dalit, Adivasis and other backward classes. The proportion of landless agricultural workers in the rural population increased from 25 per cent in 1981 to over 40 per cent in 2002. This indicates the growing pauperization of the poorer sections of the peasantry and their growing alienation from land, which forces them to join the ranks of landless agricultural labourers. The average number of days of work available to an agricultural worker in a year slumped from 123 a year in the 1980s to 78 in the 1990s. "Growing unemployment and loss of jobs in the wake of deteriorating economic conditions over the past 10 years or more under the reforms regime have also added to the misery of the poor."[6]

NSS data show that the annual growth rate of rural employment has plunged from 2.03 per cent between 1987–88 and 1993–94 to just 0.58 per cent between 1993–94 and 1999–2000. A large number of retrenched workers from the cities have returned to the villages and have added to the number of rural unemployed. The reduction in rural employment schemes by the central and state governments have also adversely affected the employment situation in the countryside. Agricultural workers are subjected to the severest forms of exploitation. The decline in public investment and the reduction of subsidies to agricultural inputs have increased the difficulties of the poor and middle peasants. They also face difficulties in getting institutional credit at affordable rates of interest and hence have to rely on moneylenders who advance loans at exorbitant rates of interest.

"While employment generation in general has been a major failure of the macro-economic policies of the past decade, the decline in agricultural employment generation has probably been the most startling."[7] The growth of agricultural employment by usual status (the number of people reporting themselves as 'usually employed') decreased to annual rate of 2.08 per cent of the period 1987–88 to 1993–1994 to only 0.8 per cent in the period of 1993–94 to 1999–2000. The fall in terms of daily status was even sharper from 2.47 per cent to 0.14 per cent in the same period. Over the 1990s, the 'weekly status' unemployment rate was around 7 per cent for men and 10 per cent for women, exceptionally high for a country with little or no protection for working people by way of social security or unemployment, compensation. Reduction in public investment, removal of quantitative restrictions on imports, squeeze on rural credit, sharply reduced expenditures on rural development and employment schemes, and the overall deflationary macro-economic policies deriving from the obsession with the reduction of the fiscal deficit—all these contributed to the sharp decline in the growth rate of employment. "... the trend in aggregate poverty incidence ... was strongly related to neo-liberal economic policies, and consequent macro-economic processes of the 1990s, these policies involved neglect of rural investment and of the food security system, resulting in slow agricultural growth, reduced employment opportunities in rural areas, and high food prices. All these would typically be likely to be associated with persistent, or even increasing poverty."[8] The noted economist V.M. Rao does not feel that policies to accelerate growth would make adequate provisions to protect the poor and enable them to grow. Growth is for those who can afford it; the poor are entitled only to poverty alleviation![9] The benefits of new economic policies go to only a marginal section—the educated urban population. The social costs in this period of globalization have been almost entirely borne by the poor and the Dalits constitute the major chunk of the lot. It is a matter of serious concern that the number of people living in poverty has increased and the levels of human development, which had improved after the 1960s have started to stagnate and even decline. The levelling of incomes that was supposed to occur with the rise in productivity, reforms and an increase in the country's shares in global trade, finance and services, has not taken place.

Conclusion

These policies of economic reforms are only the extended fingers of the process of corporate globalization desperately prospecting worldwide for new markets and ways of keeping the super-profits going. These are policies of global control over India's vast resources and markets.

The capital influx in the rural areas will have naturally in the rich farmers who have hegemonic hold over their areas. These sections, will be the main beneficiaries of the improved terms of trade and capitalist development in the rural areas. All the Dalits would be thrown into the job market along with many non-Dalit marginal to middle farmers. The vast army of unemployed thus created by this developmental dynamics will need appropriate instruments for being controlled. The history bears ample testimony to the fact that whenever the people tended to come together with a common identity, the ruling classes have deftly used the time-tested weapon of castes to divide them. Unlike elsewhere, the reforms thus are likely to enliven and rejuvenate the archaic value system.

Unless, there is a widespread purchasing power in the economy the market can never be free and sustainable. The reform strategy thus should embody sustainable economic empowerment of rural masses; investments to enhance their capability and effective measures for accelerated development of the disadvantaged sections like Dalits. The prerequisite to reform, therefore, could be the radical land reforms, massive investments in rural areas into agriculture-related infrastructural projects, universalization of primary education, primary healthcare system and reinforcement of positive discrimination in favour of Dalits. The devil of casteism could be tamed only by freeing general masses of people from the anxieties and uncertainties about basic survival.

Notes

1. C.P. Chandrashekhar and Jayati Ghosh, *The Market that Failed: A Decade of Neo-Liberal Economic Reforms in India,* Leftword Books, New Delhi, 2002.
2. Guy Standing, Director of the ILO's Socio-Economic Security Programme, *Frontline*, November 5, 2004, p. 80.
3. Anand Teltumbde, in a paper presented in a seminar organized by University of Oxford, Oxford on November 8, 1996, via internet.
4. National Human Rights Commission Report on "Prevention of Atrocities against Scheduled Castes" (2002), authored by K.B. Saxena, retired IAS officer.
5. NHRC Report cited above.
6. NHRC Report.
7. Jayati Ghosh, "Whatever Happened to Farm Employment?" *Frontline*, May 23, 2003.
8. C.P. Chandrashekhar and Jayati Ghosh, *The Market that Failed: A Decade of Neo-liberal Economic Reforms in India*, Leftword Books, New Delhi, 2002.
9. G.S. Aurora, (ed.), *Poverty and Economic Reforms: The Social Concerns,* Academic Foundation in association with Institute for Social and Economic Change, New Delhi, (2004).

11

Policy of Economic Liberalization: Its Impact on Dalits

RATNESH KISHORE VERMA AND G.M. MUSTAFA

Liberalization is the new buzzword that has come to dominate the world since the nineties of the last century.[1]

The policy of economic liberalization and its impact on Dalits have given rise to question of far-reaching substantial and procedural importance.[2] Liberalization call for a rolling back of the state on economic issues which necessitates a re-defining of state's new role and reexamining of its structures and processes. Liberalization means a clear subordination of the domestic to global and international, indicating a containment of space available to domestically defiend and democratically shaped politics. Quest for liberalization has seen reemergence of complex framework of trade negotiation—GATT, WTO, MIGA, TRIMS, TRIPS and so on. And state have been instrumental in binding economics and market of specific region.[3] State is expected to take active interest in improving conditions of Dalits through intervention for the growth of markets.[4]

The word 'Dalit' relates to the settlement of disputes through judicial bodies. It is in this respect that the term Dalit has a positive character. A new awareness has developed that informs that the rights of Dalit or an individual should be reasonably restricted in the wider interest of his community so that the ends of social justice are properly achieved.

Here the question, what are the impacts on Dalit through economic liberalization? I code, ... the idea of social justice envisages to promote the welfare of the people by securing and developing a just social and economic order. It is true to say that the national integration can be preserved through ideal social and economic justice sustained efforts are to be made in this direction by politicians, planners, administrators, jurists and social workers.

Basic tenets of liberalization carry a reform agenda which includes flexibility in the hiring and firing of workers, the freedom of entry of capital, the ready availability of land for new business activities and adequate infrastructure. The ending of state monopolies in banking, insurance and telecoms, the transfer of ownership of state-owned enterprises to private owners and the closure of loss-making state firms come in addition to unshackling the private sector. Trade liberalization, foreign direct investment, private financing of infrastructure, tax reforms, financial enterprises, labour law reforms, land law reforms and a reorientation of government social policy are major aspects of the process of liberalization.[5] Its ultimate aim is of integration with the Indian economy.

States have tended to disown responsibility towards meeting the basic needs of citizens, riding on this has come the transfer of major responsibility to the NGO sector. Many responsibilities and resources have been transferred to this sector in order to manage the social costs of transition towards liberalization.[6] However, corruption has come to characterize the NGO sector too. Liberalization does not imply decentralization, but replacement of state power by the power of corporate interests of centralized control of powerful NGOs of exogenous origin. It has resulted into dilution of foundational principles of accountability and democracy. Growing power of exogenous forces (dominant political and economic powers in the global political economy) over the economic forces of nations is its real intent.

However, the net results of liberalization for economy of the Dalit indicate negative fallouts. It has not altered these economies, but has also violently oriented them towards elitist interests, exclusion and marginaliztion of resource poor, and unsustainable face of development. People suffer on account of growing unemployment as a result of the growing thrust towards technology oriented production processes either for exports or because of the pressure to compete with increasing imports due to opening up of economy or simply due to availability of cheap labour displacing technology.

The latest trends are undoubtedly towards market economy and de-bureaucratization, downsizing, disinvestments, privatization and globalization. However, empirical evidences suggest that increasing role of private sector and NGOs in increasing goods and services are not proving satisfactory. Putting great emphasis on outsourcing and contracting out of public services involves overlooking of social concerns. Public good components should continue to be an important social aspect of government business. Collective public interest should in no case be ignored. Widespread inequalities and lack of purchasing power make privatization a poor option in most Third World countries. Bidding goodbye to welfares is not in the interest of vast masses. So, the goals of the New World Order in the wake of the changing demands of the future civilization should be human rights, human development, empowerment of people, gender equity and care for non-humans and concern for future generations.

Notes

1. S.L. Gupta, "Globalization and the State", *Indian Journal of Political Science*, Vol. 62 (3), September 2001, p. 293.
2. R.B. Jain, "Globalization, Market Economy and Human Security", *Indian Journal of Public Administration*, Vol. 13 (3), July-September 1996, pp. 312–13.
3. Dolly Arora, "Politics, Markets and Social Concerns: Liberalization and Reorganization of Space", *Indian Journal of Public Administration*, Vol. 13 (3), July-September 1996, p. 285.
4. World Bank, World Development Report, 1996.
5. Jaffery Sach, *India's Unfinished Reforms Agenda*, ICRIERE, Delhi 1994.
6. C.S. Paul and A. Israel, (eds.), *Non-Government Organization and World Bank.*

12

New Economic Policy: Its Impact on Dalits

JAINENDRA YADAV

"In pursuance and compulsion of international institutions and agreements, the Indian government had introduced several new economic measures both in the spheres of liberalization of its trade with other countries and structural adjustment of its own economy, partially in the mid-eighties and more comprehensively in the early 1990s. This process of so-called reform is still continuing with full vigour. These measures have now come to be known as New Economic Policy. These measures are new in so far as they reverse the main, if not all the policy instruments used by the government since the beginning of the planning in the early 1950s."[1] The introduction of the New Economic Policy (NEP) in 1991, otherwise known as the 'Structural Adjustment Programme (SAP)' was a manifestation of the state's strong commitment to solving prolonged economic crises, poverty and political instability. The policy shifted Indian economic policy from Nehruvian socialism towards a new open market economy. A standardized package of neo-liberal economic policies designed by the World Bank and IMF was implemented. It included devaluation of Indian currency, privatization of public enterprises and the liberalization of trade.[2&3]

On the international trade front, India has provided market access and liberalized flow in the case of about 760 commodities, similar access is allowed in capital investment and flow both ways. International companies are allowed in insurance and other services. In domestic economy SAP is introduced which mainly include (a) privatization of public sector and service, (b) liberalization in the form of removing the restriction on private sectors, and (c) withdrawal of the state from many sectors and therefore reduction of government role.

In so far as the new economic policy is based on the premises of free trade, private sector and the markets, it implied a drastic reduction in the economic and social role of the government, and hence, the policies and programmes, which have been built up by the wider participation of the state during the 1950s to 1980s are being completely reversed. Some of these policies, were devised keeping in view the interest of the labour, the poor and the social downtrodden classes like Dalits. In so far as these policies are being reversed, the new policies are going to create adverse economic consequences for the labour, poor and particularly, the Dalits.

Position of Dalits

Dalits are the most marginalized section of the Indian society. They share poverty with other poor section in Indian society, but additionally and more importantly also suffer from exclusion and immense discrimination in economic spheres—in market and out side market. They suffer from discrimination on the basis of descent and occupation. In this sense, the excluded groups as the Dalits constitute a sizable section in India, Nepal, Bangladesh and Sri Lanka, and also the Buraku from Japan and similar groups from African countries. In India alone the Dalit account about 17 per cent (equivalent to 1,382 million) of India's population in 1991, (estimate for 2001 put this figures at 18%). If we include other discriminated Dalit groups such as Dalit Christians, Dalit Sikhs and others, the number would go up to nearly one-fourth of India's population.

Dalits, at the lowest end of the economic and social ladder, are quite obviously at the receiving end of the elitist culture promoted by globalization. Dalits constitute the vast majority of the low income tier in India and have been placed at the bottom of the socio-economic and political strata.[4&5]

It is an open truth that Dalits, one of the most oppressed and repressed strata anywhere in the history of world, are still reeling under the avaricious chains of casteism. In the Indian context, social system based on caste has its deep felt impact not only on the socially but at large politically, economically, culturally, intellectually and psychologically. In world history, India is the only nation with the longest history of oppression and suppressed on the basis of varna and caste. This deprives the Dalits and other marginalized communities their right to land, work, education, health facilities, rights over natural resources and so on.

New Economic Policy and Dalits

Globalization has already brought in far-reaching changes, throwing to the winds, the earlier pretensions and legitimacy of the state and the political system that controls the state. In the Indian context too, this policy of breaking the community has worked. Apart from operating this primary objective, it has succeeded in weaning away the people from all sorts of resources. Employment ratio is on a decline. All PSUs are either closed down or handed over to the corporate sector. Privatization has become the buzzword of globalization. Market has become the 'god' of the ruling elite. The prophets of liberalization, privatization and globalization claims of creating new job opportunities, but what we have seen in the last one decade is entirely the opposite and a matter of deliberate concern. Clarion call of the capitalistic system has entangled Dalits and other hampered sections without much of options. When the Dalits demand for reservation in private sector they are rejected and under the aegis of incompetent and unskilled. This again is another trap to reduce the space of Dalits. Hence, the rich are becoming richer and poor are pushed beyond the margins. No appropriate measures have been taken to provide employment for the already marginalized strata in any way. Contrary to this, these forces had taken their land and other resources away and their life conditions have further deteriorated.[6]

Isolation, exclusion, discrimination and other forms of caste oppression is still vibrant in its crude form leading to powerlessness, helplessness, remorselessness and indignity of the already battered strata. Unfortunately, the Indian state has not made any serious attempt even after independence, which apparently stratifies the caste character of the state. The modest space generated through reservation is at stake and has been considered as an offering in the beggar's bowl not as the right of Dalits. No doubt, this is the historical fascism that Dalits have been faced with.

Such macro-economic policy changes have certain negative outcomes, especially in regards to the poor and disadvantaged like the Dalits. Ongoing economic reform continues to increase prices and unemployment, and the reduction and elimination of all subsidies and social sector expenditures has further worsened the economic situation for the Dalits.[7]

The spirit built by Ambedkar, while amending the Constitution, has not only tattered away but a much stronger appearance of casteism is being manifested. Even the little openings and space created through Mandal Commission is at the verge of extinction. It is only a matter of time for the final rites. In the private sector, when Dalits demand for reservation they are denied of their rights under the aegis of unfit and incompetent. This argument again is untrue and misleading that Dalits are unskilled and inefficient.

Rather than addressing the elementary problems like landlessness, unemployment, powerlessness, education and health facilities of Dalits, it is diversifying the attention to which there is utmost encouragement given by the present state. No actions to ensure any of these aspects have yet come into existence despite 57 years of independence. On the other hand, there are statements and claims from the government that they have been engaged for the betterment of the Dalits at large in the state. Many projects and programmes are initiated with tremendous flow of fund. Yet, Dalits are poor, powerless, resourcesless and victimized by caste system.

As a community we are in crisis—the crisis of life, the crisis of disharmony, the crisis of livelihood, the crisis of sustainability and so on. It is not that we were not in any sort of crisis before but today the crisis has expanded to unpredictable magnitude with severe implication and utter insinuation and the state is helpless.

"Theoretically quite simply, I term it as imperialist globalization and communal fascism. This is what is going on in India for more than a decade. However, the grounds were prepared even before. Fascism is a terrible political domination capable of infringing people's life to unpredictable magnitude. History has witnessed various forms of fascism that turned inertly against the already broken people. The threat of fascism remains long among the people without giving any opportunity for response to such a brutish system.

Today, globalization is not just confined to India, it has become a global fact and its direct impact is crushing all across the world. In India, it is closely associated with the process of communal fascism".[8] Globalization is ragging over the people, exclusively over the marginalized strata. State has turned out to be a feasible instrument in the hands of the corporate sector in legitimizing the concentration of wealth in MNCs and TNCs. Even the minimum space provided for Dalits through reservation has been constantly shrinking by virtue of privatization and other manifestations of globalization.

The reforms have already resulted in freezing the grants to many institutions and in stagnating, if not lowering, the expenditure on education. The free market ethos has entered the educational sphere in a big way. Commercialization of education is no more a mere rhetoric; it is now the established fact. Commercial institutions offering specialized education signifying the essential input from utilitarian viewpoint have come up in a big way from cities to small towns. Their product prices are not only based on the demand-supply consideration in their market segment but also are manipulated by their promotional strategies. In a true spirit of globalization, many foreign universities are invading the educational spheres through hitherto unfamiliar strategic alliances with non-descript commercial agencies, of course at hefty dollar equivalent prices. Many elite institutions like IIMs, IITs and suddenly facing fund crunch had to raise their fee structure and other prices manifold. They were already beyond the reach of Dalits. When they eventually turn self-financing, their prices would be benchmarked against their international counterparts, which anyway would be affordable to the same top market segment that constitutes the focus of all the reform-talk. As the job markets become acutely competitive, owing to a sharp decline in job opportunities, the polarization between the elite and commoner has sharpened. Various kinds of price barriers would be erected to thwart the entry of downtrodden.

Even the sphere of primary education, the coverage of which has been so miserably inadequate as to leave out multitude of children in villages as illiterate, could not remain unaffected, notwithstanding its already existing divide between the vernacular and English schools. Corporatization has entered this arena, transforming the education into an enterprise for profits. Today, educational sector is more commonly known as education industry. The quality of input these expensive schools provide will benchmark the products in the contracting job markets. Even today, because of preponderance of the English language in business circles, the divide between village and towns is almost complete in the field of education. It is so difficult for a village student, educated in vernacular medium to compete with his convent-educated counterpart in cities and towns. If this is the situation of general village population, the plight of Dalits who besides being the poorest of the village population carry additional Bretton Woods of social discrimination, is indeed a worrisome matter. Despite several kinds of state assistance, Dalits are plagued with alarming rate of school dropouts. This may be explained out as much by the need for Dalit children to supplement their meagre family incomes for meeting the two ends as also the erosion of their faith that education could be the instrument to change the pathetic course of their lives. This sense of alienation is going to grow with the progress of the reforms.

Conclusion

Whatever may be the other costs, the government policy of reservations in employment sphere has undoubtedly played an important role for Dalits. Howsoever unsatisfactory the results of the implementation may be, the importance of reservations from the Dalit viewpoint cannot be overemphasized. As could be evidenced by the organized private sector, where it would be difficult to find a Dalit employee (save of course in scavenging and menial jobs), without reservations, Dalits would have been totally doomed. The winds of privatization under the economic reforms have already shaken the very foundations of the reservations. The reforms clearly envisage the minimalist government. Wherever the reforms patterned on the SAP of the World Bank were carried out, denationalization of the public sector and privatization have come in a big way. Whatever the scenario, the residual structures of the 'reformed' PSUs are never going to be the same, as far as Dalits are concerned. The ethos of privatization and the excuse of competition, superimposed on the traditional caste prejudice, will never allow reservations to happen, any more.

In simple terms the economics of Dalits is simply related to that of being powerless and resourceless, both socially and politically. The very historical status of Dalits is continued and perpetuated by the new models of capitalism. They are landless. With the dramatic savior like entrance of new economic policy through the structural adjustment programme the minimum substantial livelihood that they used to have is also diffusing. Their social disabilities, largely reinforced by and sustained on the economic deprivations, are bound to get accentuated with these policies.[9]

Notes

1. Sukhadeo Thorat, Indian Institute of Dalit Studies, Jawaharlal Nehru University, New Delhi, 'Dalits and Globalization'. The presentation was delivered at the World Social Forum held in Mumbai.
2. R. Dewan, "Gender Implications of the New Economic Policy: A Conceptual Overview", *Women's Studies International Forum*, Vol. 22, No. 4, 1999.
3. U.D. Upadhyay, "India's New Economic Policy of 1991 and its Impact on Women's Poverty and AIDS", *Feminist Economics*, Vol. 6, No. 3, 2000.
4. P. Appasamy, *UNDP Research Series*, 1996.
5. John and Lalita, Overseas Development Administration, London, February 1995.
6. Kothari, Minogue and Dejong, "The Political Economy of Globalization" in Kothari and Minogue (eds.), *Development Theory and Practice: Critical Perspectives,* Hampshire: Palgrave, 2002.
7. Fernando, "Non-Governmental Organizations, Micro-Credit and Empowerment of Women", Annals, *AAPSS*, 554, November 1997.
8. Goldy George, "The Dalit World of Injustice and Peacelessness" via Internet.
9. Goldy George, ibid.

13

Globalization and Its Impact on Dalits

CHITRA PRABHAT

The multifaceted social system of India based on caste, which believed to be historically engineered by the orthodox higher caste Hindus, still is in vigour even after five decades of India's independence, despite many efforts by the social formers and notwithstanding implementation of various laws and amendments to abolish the caste hierarchies.

Globalization has brought immense changes in the social cultural life of Indians during the last two decades. Some scholars argue that globalization has not been successful in liberating the people from the oppression and it was totally directed towards elite class, others viewed that globalization has significant effect on Dalits to bring them into the mainstream culture. In fact as far as global, culture is concerned, the Dalit culture is a part of the global culture and therefore it is obvious that Dalit culture has effective share in some part of global culture.

The doctrinal basis of today's globalization is provided by the 'neo-liberalism' that represented revival of economic liberalism propounded by Adam Smith in 1776 in his famous book titled, *Wealth of Nations*. Economic liberalism advocated the abolition of the government matters; it considered free trade was the best way for a nation's economy to develop. These ideas were liberal in the sense of no controls. The Bretton Woods institutions have been the main instrument to spread the wings of globalization. However, it can be adopted by every nation, state in the form of some kind of local initative euphemistically called as reforms. These economic reforms were launched in July 1951 in India.

Globalization is the creation of a new global culture with its attendant social structures, one which increasingly becomes the broader social context of all particular cultures in the world, including those of the West. Globalization therefore in a single word can be called as the homogenization of all cultures into one single culture. For Robertson, globalization refers to the "overall process by which the entire world becomes increasingly interdependent, so as to yield a 'single place'. We could even go far as to call the latter as 'world society', as long as we do not suggest by the term that nationally constituted societies are disappearing". Other scholars define globalization as the expansion of market economy and spread of global culture by replacing or supplementing the localized culture.

Dalits have made a significant progress on almost all parameters during the five post-independent decades. Out of total Dalit population of 138 million, the number of Dalits in services falling in the domain of reservation does not exceed 1.1 million, i.e., a mere 0.8 per cent.

Dalit, the very term, is derived from the Sanskrit root 'dal' which means burst, split, broken or torn asunder, downtrodden, scattered crushed, destroyed. The word was first used by British, then by B.R. Ambedkar in his Marathi speech, "The Untouchables" published in 1948. Later, the Dalit Panthers revived the term in their 1973 manifesto extending its definition to include scheduled tribes, neo-Buddhists, the working people, the landless and poor peasants women and all those who are being exploited politically, economically and in the name of religion. Dalit communities in India are extremely heterogeneous groups having divided into hundreds of castes, sub-castes and sub-subcastes and spread in every nook and corner of India.

Dalits who are socially weak, economically and physically poor and politically powerless have changed today as the Dalits raised their voices and claimed their social identity as never before few decades ago.

The process of globalization through TV, radio, cinema, internet and other sources has made tremendous impact on the life and culture of Dalits. It is true that globalization has created opportunities and economic growth, employment and variety of goods. The economic structure adopted by the Dalits of today has immense importance in understanding the changes that have taken place in their traditional caste structure. Today, the life pattern has gone upward mobility. Better economic opportunity, better communication facility and exposure to the mass media, etc. have reinforced the motivation of Dalits to achieve higher social status.

In the rural area globalization has done little for the improvement in the quality of life of the poor rather it has given them the taste of consumerism by sending a plethora of consumer goods which has little to do with their quality of life. State withdrawal from public services has resulted in contributing an unethical ill-educated rural populace to the existing pool of unemployed. Globalization strategy has negatively affected the poor, in general and the Dalit, in particular.

The impact of globalization on Dalit can be assessed along several dimensions but here the study confines itself to the three most predominant ones, viz., social status, employment and reservation in services.

In social terms, all Dalits irrespective of their economic standing in rural areas, but in urban areas they have made significant progress. They are scattered in different areas and have formed their own colonies. They celebrate all Hindu pujas. Now, during the time of marriage, they are invited in order to beat drums or dholos, to play *Madhuries* (flutes) and so on. Today, modernization has however changed one of the major occupations of Dalits in India, i.e., the job of scavengers.

The rate of growth of employment in the organized sector dropped from more than 1.2 per cent per annum in the late 1992–93 to 0.6 per cent in 2002–03. Creation of jobs in public sector fell, for the private sector it showed a slight rise from 2.08 million to 2.49 million on account of free market euphoria.

There is a picture of declining employment opportunity and appointments. The contraction in public expenditure and the consequent reduction in aggregate demand could not but adversely affect employment in the unorganized sector. Whether non-agricultural rural employment or urban informal sector employment given the casual nature of such employment. Opportunities for Dalits and backwards in the organized sectors have reduced as historically due to bias and lack of sufficient qualifications required for obtaining employment in the private sector. The training is highly expensive because education system is privatize. A simultaneous operation of privatization has closed the door as a provider of employment, in general and the Dalits in particular, play an effective role.

Whatever may be the other costs but the government policy of reservation in employment sphere has undoubtedly played an important role in the process of advancement of the Dalits. The winds of privalization under the economic reforms have already shaken the very foundations of reservations. The reforms clearly envisage the minimalist state wherever the reforms patterned on the structural adjustment programme of the World Bank were carried out, denationalization and privatization of the public sector have come in a big way. Being a late starter, India has not reached the scales achieved by others, say, the Latin American countries. However the start has not been any less impressive within a short time, almost all the sectors of economy stand opened up for private investment. The disinvestment in existing public sector companies has already been allowed up to 49 per cent by the policy. The public stake being more than 50 per cent, the public sector as such is not yet dismantled in the policy. It continues to be the state, before, and hence attracts application of the reservation policy. However, the reform package has already endangered, if not abolished, the reservations through numerous back doors.

Reservation in the educational institutions and the financial assistance in the form of scholarships and freeships constitute perhaps the most important factor in the development scheme for Dalits. For, it is primarily responsible to make the basic input of education available and affordable to them. Without education all the constitutional safeguards including reservation in services would be infractuous. The free market ethos has entered the educational sphere in a big way. Commercialization of education is no more a mere rhetoric, it is now the established fact. Commercial institutions offering specialized education that signify essential input from utilitarian viewpoint have come big way from cities to small towns. Their product prices are not only based on the demand-supply consideration in their market segment but also are manipulated by their promotional strategies. In a true sprit of globalization many foreign universities are invading the educational spheres through hitherto unfamiliar strategic alliances with non-descript commercial agencies. Many elite institutions like IIMs and IITs suddenly facing fund crunch had to resort to raising their fee structure and other prices manifold. They were already beyond the reach of the Dalits.

Even in the sphere of primary education the coverage of which has been so miserably inadequate as to leave out multitude of children in villages as illiterate, could not remain unaffected, notwithstanding its already existing divide between the vernacular and English school corporation has entered this arena transforming the education into an enterprise for profits. The quality of input these expensive school provide will benchmark the products in the contracting job markets. Even today, because of preponderance of the English language in business circles, the divide between village and towns is almost complete in the field of education. It is so difficult for a village student especially of weaker section and Dalits to get education in this environment.

The broad Indian reality is that India has too many poor even today. India is predominantly an agrarian economy with over 70 per cent of its population living in villages. There are inequalities not only in economic terms but also in the socio-cultural terms.

Globalization has introduced to India new technology and economic opportunities and greater sensitivity to efficiency. But it is true that globalization increases economic and political inequalities but every dark cloud has a silver lining.

References

Bayer, Peter, *Religion and Globalization,* Sage Publications, London, 1994, p. 9

Bhattacharya, M. (1994), "Impact of Liberalization on Small Scale Sector", Office of the Development Commissioner, India, New Delhi, *EPW*, p. 1312.

Dani, Rodrik, (1999), *Has Globalization Gone Too Far?* Washington D.C., Institute for International Economics.

Kumar, Raj, "Dalit Culture: A Perspective from Below", *Social Action*, Vol. 50, No. 1, Jan-March 2000.

Kurien, C.T., (1996), "The Real Impact", *Frontline*, February 9, p. 97.

Poddar, Bhagirath, *The Untouchables in Modern India,* Sarup and Sons Publication, New Delhi, 2001, p. 53.

Robertson, Ronald, "Internationalization and Globalization" University Centre for International Studies, Newsletter, University of Pittsburgh, 1989, pp. 8–9.

Singh, Ajit Kumar, (1993), "Social Consequences of New Economic Policy", *Economic and Political Weekly*, February 13.

14

New Economic Policy and Its Economic Impact on Dalits

GOPAL KUMAR SINGH

The economic reforms launched in July 1991, in India, were in nature of a crisis management response to the economic and political crises that erupted in early 1991. The economic crisis comprised a steep fall in the foreign exchange reserve, galloping inflation, large public and current account deficits and mounting Bretton Woods of domestic and foreign departments. In politics, the fall of two governments in a short span of four months, from November 1990 to March 1991; deferment of presentation of the union budget, fairly long political interregnum till the elections, the assassination of a former Prime Minister Rajiv Gandhi in the midst and the emergence of a minority government with a leader sans charisma, reflected an unprecedented crisis. These events led to a sharp erosion of confidence in India among leaders, downgradation of India's credit rating and consequently cut of international credit lines from private or commercial sources. Indian reforms thus, were essentially of a 'crisis-driven' variety. They did not represent strategic choice with a vision of long-term development of Indian people.

The term 'New Economic Policy' (NEP) is a signification of the process of dismantling 'licence-permit-subsidy Raj' and to infuse liberalization in the management of the economy. It is imperative to point out that economic liberalization does not mean laissez-faire. In fact, the NEP is based on the premise that all the interventionist policies may not be desirable. Hence, the NEP seeks to scrap the undesirable restrictions, controls and licensing over investment, imports and production. Ashok V. Desai has aptly summed up the philosophy of NEP: "One must first get clear about what liberalization involved. What it involved was a relaxation of bureaucratic controls on the allocations of resources."

The main ingredients of the NEP may be spelled out as follows:

1. restoration of competition;
2. progressive dismantling of industrial licensing system;
3. liberalization of trade regime and ushering in a new era of competitiveness in imports and exports;
4. re-orientation of fiscal policy;
5. necessary amendment in the Monopolies and Restrictive Trade Practices (MRTP) Act to enable the larger business houses to invest their resources in industries which are of national importance and for which smaller companies could not muster sufficient funds to invest;
6. liberalization of policy regime for direct foreign investment and foreign technology agreements;
7. a bigger role for the private sector;
8. technological upgradation in all the spheres of economic activities to 'take the country to 21st century'; and
9. a long-term perspective instead of frequent changes in the areas of fiscal, import and export policies.

In short, the New Economic Policy's thrust is on insulation the Indian economy from bureaucratic impediments to industrial growth by relaxation of controls.

Dalits in India

Dalits, as the ex-untouchables prefer to be called, are a very distinct social group. While belonging to a broad class of have-nots they suffer an additional disability of social oppression. Economically, most of them are still the poorest of poor. The balance minuscule minority has managed to escape poverty limits and to locate itself on to continuum ranging up to a reasonable level of prosperity. The main factor that has catalyses this transition is the reservation policy, all Dalits, irrespective of their economic standing, still suffer oppression. This social oppression varies from the crudest variety of untouchability still being practised in rural areas, to the sophisticated forms of discrimination encountered even in modern sectors of urban areas. Although, the statistics indicate that Dalits have made a significant progress on almost all parameters during the five post-independence decades, the relative distance between them and non-Dalits seems to have remained the same or increased. More than 75 per cent of the Dalit workers are still connected with land; 25 per cent being the marginal and small farmers and balance over 50 per cent are the landless labourers. In urban areas, they work mainly in unorganized sector. Out of the total Dalit population of 250 million, the number of Dalits in services falling in the domain of reservations does not exceed 1.1 million; a mere 0.8 per cent.

Dalits in India are 250 million people, which is more than the population of Canada, Australia, Sweden and Belgium together. We do not find a suffering mass as big as that in any part of the world as we do in India. This massive group of human beings has been suffering for the last 2,000 years merely because they were born in the lowest rung of the caste system. Dalits and their subjugation are a product of the Hindu caste system. For the understanding of my readership, I would like to mention the basic characteristics of caste here.

As per the definition given by one of the authorities on the study of the caste system, Dr Ketkar, "Caste is a social group having two characteristics: (i) Membership (of a particular caste) is confined to those who are born of members and includes all persons so born. (ii) The members are forbidden by an inexorable social law to marry outside the group". Caste is also recognized as varna of Varnasharama Dharma of the Hindu religion. Caste of varna was created as a vertical hierarchical division of the society. Brahmins were placed at the top of the system and the Dalits were placed at the bottom; Dalits actually formed the fifth varna, which is lower in status than the fourth varna. The people under the fourth varna, known as Shudras, were sufficiently degraded in the religious books;

one can imagine the situation of the people who were another step below the Shudras. That is why, the Dalits have another name called, 'outcaste'. Dalits were deprived of the basic human rights, the right to education and their degraded position was sanctified by the religious law books. Here are two verses from the testes of the Hindu religion:

> Now if a Shudra listens intentionally to (a recitation of) the Veda, his ears shall be filled with (molten) tin or lac (*Gauttam Dharma Sutra 124*).

Vedas were the first religious books of the Hindus. Hindus or Brahmins to be precise, declared Vedas as divine and hence, infallible. Another verse is:

> If a Sudra recites (Vedic text), his tongue shall be cut out (*Gautam Dharma Sutra 125*).

Hindu religious books are full of such discriminatory and derogatory rulings for the Dalits. The above two verses are just enough to illustrate the point. The official name, a dopted by the Constitution of India, for the Dalits is Scheduled Castes (SC–15% of India's population) and Scheduled Tribes (ST–7.5% of India's population). Prior to India's independence, Dalits were identified by different names like untouchables, depressed classes, outcastes, etc. Different names could appear in this paper for Dalits, but they represent the same people.

Having understood the background of the Dalits and the pernicious caste system, we now come back to the topic of what damage the NEP of liberalization has done to the advancement of Dalits.

Impact of the NEP on Dalits

The social disadvantage suffered by Dalits in India was taken care of in the Constitution of India which was drafted under the chairmanship of Dr Ambedkar—a person who had spearheaded the most momentous anti-caste movement of the depressed classes. It provided Dalits with many safeguards, viz., (i) social, educational, cultural and religious safeguards, (ii) economic safeguards, (iii) political safeguards, and (iv) safeguards for the Indian Constitution of 'one vote, one value', nor can it coexist with the system of positive discrimination embodied in these safeguards. For the market grants moneyed person more value, and overtly believes in the jungle law of 'might is right'. To a large extent, the primary motivation behind these constitutional provisions was liberal democratic aspiration that characterized the freedom movement. However, these aspirations and the initial ideological zeal of the founding fathers withered away in no time and what survived was its utilitarian dimension for the electoral politics. The sorry state of the executive compliance with these constitutional provisions amply bears out the fangs of the Indian society. The reforms will bring a kind of legitimacy to this attitudinal resistance. These safeguards will stand eroded as the reforms gain in momentum. Influence of the reforms is bound to be all pervasive. However, only a few issues of importance to the Dalit masses have been picked up for discussion here.

The main thrust of the NEP was on liberalization, privatization and globalization (LPG). NEP was planned in two phases: (1) by the devaluation of Indian rupees by 20 per cent, and (2) by the long-term, Structural Adjustment Programme (SAP). In essence, the NEP planned to achieve progressive reduction of the role of the 'state' in the economic management of the country and move the 'centrally planned' Indian economy to a 'free market' economy. This looks nice for a state that does not have social disparities. India, since its independence in 1947 was playing the vital role of a welfare state to even out its 2,000-year-old social disparities created by the Hindu caste system. Though this was progressing at a very slow pace against the wishes of the Brahminical administration, it was making positive contributions to the development of 250 million Dalits. However, the NEP had decided to cut the role of a welfare state drastically as it decided to move towards a free market economy. India had to go a long long way to go to establish social equality. This shift in its economic policy has hampered its progress of the social equality form, which is so important and is a prerequisite for taking up to ethos of free market.

Those who are worst affected by the launching of the NEP are the Dalits who form 25 per cent of India's population. Another 50 per cent of India's population known as Other Backward Classes (OBCs) was also not in anyway ready for the NEP. The literacy rate of India at the time of the launch of NEP was merely about 50 per cent (52.14%). With about half of the population not having attained literacy, India was not ready for the economic reforms. It should not have given up its role as a welfare state until it has developed the people on vital services like education, health, etc.

The impact of NEP on Dalits was clearly visible almost immediately in terms of

1. decline in rural non-agricultural employment and income,
2. decline in the per capita availability of food grains and cereals,
3. reduction in central expenditure on anti-poverty programmes, and
4. decline in expenditure on sector which improve social consumption (Jogdand, 2000).

Reservations in Services

Whatever may be the other costs, the government policy of reservations in employment sphere has undoubtedly played an important role for Dalits. The policy broadly envisages representation of Dalits in proportion to their population in all the public services which includes the government, public sector, autonomous bodies and institutions receiving grant-in-aid from the government. A cursory glance at the figures of this representation is enough to get a pathetic state of implementation.

Howsoever, unsatisfactory the results of the implementation may be, the importance of reservations from the Dalit viewpoint cannot be overemphasized. As could be evidenced by the organized private sector, where it would be difficult to find a Dalit employee (save of course in scavenging and menial jobs), without reservations Dalits would have been totally doomed. The importance of reservations thus, could only be assessed in relation to situations where they do not exist. Whatever be their defects and deficiencies, they have given certain economic means of livelihood and some social prestige to the sons and daughters of over 1.5 million landless labourers. Whether they get real power or not, over 50,000 Dalits could enter the sphere of bureaucratic authority with the help of reservations. Besides these tangible benefits promised by the policy, it has instilled a hope in Dalit community. This hope predominantly manifests in the form of spread of education among them. Their emotional bond with the nation and its Constitution despite heaps of injustice and ignominy they bear every moment of their life may also be significantly attributable to the reservation policy.

The winds of privatization under the economic reforms have already shaken the very foundations of the reservations. The reforms clearly envisage the minimalist government. Wherever the reforms patterned on the structural adjustment programme of the World Bank were carried out, denationalization of the public sector and privatization have come in a big way. Being the late starter, India has not reached the scales achieved by others, say, the Latin American countries. However, the start has not been any unimpressive. Almost all sectors of economy stand opened up for private investment. The disinvestments in existing public sector companies has already been allowed upto 49 per cent by the policy. The public stake being more than 50 per cent, the public sector as such is not yet dismantled in policy. It continues to be the state, as before, and hence attracts application of the reservation policy. However, the reform package has already endangered, if not abolished, the reservations through back doors.

Employment

One of the main thrusts of the NEP was the shift towards privatization. To achieve the target of a free market economy, the public sector elements are required to be minimized and replaced by the private sector. In India, the share of the public sector in the total economy was less than 30 per cent (based on GDP data of 1989–90) (Jogdand, 2000). This means that the Indian economy is basically private sector controlled. Contrary to this, the share of the public sector in employment is much bigger than the private sector. In 1991, 18.97 million were employed in the public sector while only 7.85 million were employed in the private sector. Thus, the share of the public sector in employment was 70.7 per cent while that of private sector was 29.3 per cent. As far as Dalits are concerned, it is a well-known fact that government services and the public sector have provided some employment, though it was nowhere near the percentage fixed by government regulations (15% for SCs and 7.5% for STs). In contrast, the private sector is extremely poor in terms of employment generation. Let us look at a comparative data of 1982–83.

In 1982–83, employment in the private sector was 7.55 million, which rose to only 7.67 million in 1990–91. During this period, the gross fixed capital formation at current market prices, which was Rs 171.83 billion rose by four times to Rs 709.33 billion and rose by two times under constant prices to Rs 346.99 billion in terms of 1980-81 prices. Thus, the rise in gross fixed capital formation in the private sector was of the order of Rs 170 billion, which resulted in 1,00,000 jobs. Gross fixed capital formation rose from Rs 238.28 billion in 1990–91 to Rs 1,785.68 billion in 1995–96 at current prices. But, the employment increased from 7.5 million in 1990 to 8 million in 1995; that is an increase of Rs 1,047.32 billion. GDFC resulted in only 0.5 million jobs during five years in the private sector. On the other hand in the public sector, gross fixed capital formation increased from Rs 50,176 billion in 1990–91 to Rs 91,703 billion at current prices in 1995–96, while employment increased from 18.77 million in 1990 to 19.46 million in 1995. That is, an increase of Rs 415.27 billion of gross fixed capital formation lead to 7,00,000 jobs (Jogdand, 2000:27). Hence, it is evident that the private sector generates much less employment compared to public sector for the same gross fixed capital formation.

As far as the 250 million Dalits are concerned, they have no place in the private sector. Private entrepreneurship, in India, has been traditionally known for being heavily prejudistic about caste Hindus, which constitute Brahmins, Kshatriyas and Vaishyas. Their methodology of recruitment is foolproof, that no Dalit can easily enter the officer category. In the last decade, few Dalits, may be a few hundred (in the officer category) have possibly entered the private sector. This has possibly happened because of high demand of certain hi-tech professions, especially in computer sciences and engineering. In such a situation, they cannot afford to look at the caste of the person. But, when the demand and supply of professionals is even, thus caste definitely plays a vital factor. Thus, so far, Dalits have been systematically kept out of the private sector.

Privatization is also being extended to social services like education and health. Then, education and health also becomes commodities. Government spendings are reduced with this plan. From Table 1, it can be seen that the budget share of the education, sanitation and child welfare declined from 26.3 per cent in 1990–91 to 23.9 per cent in 1994–95. The outlay for SC/ST and OBC welfare has also declined from 8 per cent of total outlay to 7.8 per cent during the same period. The implementation of the NEP of 1990–91, has led to the decline in the employment of SCs in the government sector. The absolute number has gone down from 0.628 million in 1991 to 0.604 million in 1991 and 1992. A similar trend as expected was observed in the matter of public sector employment for SCs. The absolute number of SCs employees in public sector has declined from 0.432 million in 1990 to 0.369 million in 1992. Their percentage share also declined from 19.54 per cent to 17.74 per cent in 1990.

Table 1

Outlay on Major Rural Development and Social Services Program Central Budgets 1990–91 to 1994–95

Financial Year	*1990–91*	*1991–92*	*1992–93*	*1993–94*	*1994–95*
Basic needs (Total)	1,059	1,345	1,361	1,934	2,254
(%)	26.3	31.3	27.5	26.3	23.9
Welfare of SC/ST/OBC (Total)	321	428	465	589	730
(%)	8.0	10.2	9.4	8.0	7.8

This demonstrates that privatization and the NEP have severely affected the progress of the weaker section of the society, the Dalits, who were steadily progressing under the welfare state. Their progress has been drastically reduced by the new economic policies. The positive discrimination policy (reservation policy) of the government of India for the Dalits is almost abolished. The NEP has turned out to be a 'handy' tool in the hands of prejudistic caste Hindus to suppress the progress of Dalits.

Impact of NEP on Rural Dalits

The scheduled castes and scheduled tribes contribute a significant portion of the poor in India. In 1991, of the total rural SC/ST workers, about 82 per cent were engaged in farm activities and the remaining 18 per cent in the non-farm activities. This division for non-SCs/STs was 75 per cent and 25 per cent respectively i.e., pattern of SCs is less diversified as compared to non-SCs/STs. Further, within agriculture, the percentage of wage labourers among SCs was nearly 50 per cent. Only 33 per cent of them were cultivators. The reverse was true for non-SCs/STs, as much as 55 per cent worked in cultivation and only 20 per cent workers were wage labourers in agriculture.

Small proportions of SC households owned or cultivate land. Among them also, as many as 73 per cent were marginal farmers with average of less then 2.5 acers of land. Another 13 per cent were landless households. So, nearly 86 per cent of SC households in 1991 were landless and near-landless households. In 1987–88, of the total SC rural households, as many as 63.14 per cent were wage labours households. This percentage is quite high compared to the 31.16 per cent of non-SCs/STs. Further, nearly 63.14 per cent of wage labours households among SCs owned some land. Thus, a substantial section of land owning households among the SCs had to resort to wage employment due to the smallness of the land that they owned.

It is well known that growing public expenditure was, in the past, mainly responsible for rapid employment growth in the rural, non-agricultural sector in the 1980s. The percentage share of rural non-farm employment in total employment increased from around 14 per cent to 17 per cent and in rural employment from 17 per cent to 22 per cent between 1977–78 and 1987–88. And this has been a major factor for reducing poverty in 1977–78 and 1987–88.

Thus, the impact of the new economic measures was mainly on the rural non-farm sector and urban sector.

Poverty

The reforms have reversed the two decades long declining trend of poverty. The rural poverty went up from the pre-reform low of 33.7 per cent to 41.7 per cent in 1992 and slightly declined to 40.2 per cent in 1993–94. The urban poverty line also showed the same trend shooting up from the pre-reform low of 36 per cent to 37.8 per cent and then coming down to 36.2 per cent.

Conclusion

The economic reforms in mould of macro-economic stabilization and structural adjustment programme of IMF and World Bank have essentially a pro-rich bias, wherever they have worsened the situation of the masses of poor people in absolute as well as relative terms. The Dalits in India being the poorest of the poor have been hit the hardest. Their social disabilities largely reenforced by and sustained on the economic deprivations are bound to get accentuated with these policies. The Indian reforms were crisis-driven and not strategy-driven. When they were adopted, the complete discourse of reforms appears to lead in equalities not only in economic terms to Dalits, but in the socio-cultural reforms too.

The Way Forward for Dalits

Dalits will have to work out their strategies afresh to cope with the situation arising out of the NEP. The frustration among Dalits already building up over a decade is now due to their marginalization. They have already started voicing their demands for diversity in the private sector. They are not the only ones who have been given the protective cover of employment in the private sector, the Affirmative Action Plan of the USA is the best example. The Bhopal Declaration has also identified diversity in all fields. Implementation of Land Reforms must be given highest priority as the majority of the Dalits live in rural areas. Central and state governments must also increase the allocation of important social services, such as primary education, health, sanitation, drinking water, rural development, roads, employment generating schemes and housing.

References

Ambedkar, B.R., *Castes in India*, n.d.

Bhaduri, A. and D. Nayyar, *The Intelligent Persons' Guide to Liberalization*, Penguin, New Delhi, 1996.

Gupta, S.P., "Economic Reforms and its Impact on Poor", *Economic and Political Weekly.*

Jogdand, P.G., (ed.), *New Economic Policy and Dalits*, Rawat Publications, Jaipur, 2000.

Mangekar, B.L., The Key to Dalits Progress, International Conference on Dalits Human Rights, London.

Michacl, S.M., *Dalits in Modern India, Vision and Values*, Vistaar Publications, n.d.

15

Agricultural Sector Reforms and Its Impact on Dalits

K.J. SINHA AND SUNIL BAJPAYEE

Agriculture still continues to be an important sector in the Indian economy. Apart from its important contribution to national income and foreign exchange earnings, it is the largest source of employment and livelihood to the Indian people. Nearly 65 per cent of our population is engaged in primary economic activities (mainly in agriculture).

The agriculture sector in India is highly iniquitous both economically and socially. The land ownership pattern is not uniform among different social groups. While scheduled castes, scheduled tribes and other backward classes (commonly categorized as Dalits) dominate in numbers, and they constitute subordinate socio-economic groups. Most of the scheduled castes, scheduled tribes and other backward classes fall in the category of either small and marginal farmers or landless agricultural/bonded labours. Economically, these groups constitute the most vulnerable sections of our society.

Since, the agricultural sector is the largest source of employment and livelihood for the Dalits, naturally there exists direct co-relation between the performance of agricultural sector and the economic well-being of these groups.

Indian agricultural policies and programmes have undergone many changes since independence. Initially, policy of land reform was initiated and implemented on productivity and equity grounds. The policy and programme of land reform has failed in achieving stated objectives of fast and equitous agricultural growth. Then we followed the policy of Green Revolution to boost agricultural growth. And it was assumed that benefits of faster agricultural growth will percolate down to the vulnerable sections of our society who are mainly small/marginal farmers or landless agricultural labourers. Opinions differ on the issue of level and degree of beneficial impact on the vulnerable section of the society.

Although, Indian agricultural sector has experienced many changes in terms of policies and programmes since independence, but with the adoption of new economic policy of 1991 and after becoming the member of WTO, a series of reform process have been started in agricultural sector, which in turn is going to have far and wide range impact on the Dalit section of the society.

The major issues related to agricultural reforms are:

1. Reduction and eventual elimination of restrictions on both internal and external trade in agricultural products.
2. Reduction and eventual elimination of input subsidies.
3. Question of minimum support price and procurement price
4. And last but not the least, putting in place intellectual property rights (IPR) regime for seeds and plant varieties and allowing transnational agri-business corporations to operate freely in the country.

Agricultural reform process is being steadily enforced although slowly because of fear of backlash from farming communities and some political outfits. The impact of agricultural reform process, in company with new economic policy, on agriculture in general and vulnerable section in particular, is proving to be detrimental.

The Dalits who constitute the major chunk of vulnerable sections in rural societies seems to have suffered most from the various ongoing reform process both in agriculture and non-agricultural sectors on the following accounts:

1. Lesser investment by government in the agricultural infrastructure in the period.
2. Lesser institutional support from the financial sector owing to financial sector reforms.
3. Gradual withdrawal of extension services provided by the government.

4. Farming community has been more subjected to shocks and uncertainties both internally and externally, a result of greater openness in agricultural sector. Instead of becoming resilient agricultural sector, more and more farmers are committing suicide. The Dalits are more vulnerable to economic and non-economic shocks because of their low asset/capital base, marginal/no land ownership, non-availability or inadequate insurance coverage, inadequate credit facilities and non-implementation of minimum wage act.

References

Bhalla, G.S. and G. Singh, (1997), "Recent Development in Indian Agriculture: A State Level Analysis", *EPW*, March 29.

Chadha, G.K., (1995), "Agricultural Production Relation in the Context of New Agriculture Technology", *IJAE*, January-March.

Gill, S.S. and J.S., Brar (1996), "Global Market and Compositeness of Indian Agriculture", *EPW*, August 10.

"Globalization and Agricultural Policy in India", *Indian Journal of Agricultural Economics*, Jan-March 1995.

Gulati, A. and Rip Landes, (2004), "Farm Sector Performance and Reform Agenda", *EPW*, August 7.

Gulati, Ashok, (1997), "Freeing Trade in Agriculture: Implications for Resource Use Efficiency and Cropping Pattern Changes", *EPW*, December 17.

Hanumantha Rao, C.H. and Ashok Gulati, (1994), Indian Agriculture: Emerging Perspectives and Policy Issues, Research paper under USAID Grant, Indian Council of Agricultural Research, New Delhi and International Food Policy Research Institute, Washington, D.C.

Nayyar, Deepak and Abhijit Sen, (1994), "International Trade and Agricultural Sector in India", *EPW*, May 14.

Parikh et al. (2003), "Growth and Welfare Consequences of Rise MSP", *EPW*, March 1.

Rath, N., (2000), "Making the Economic Transition Smooth", *EPW*, May.

Vaidyanathan, (2000), "India's Agricultural Development Policy", *EPW*, May, 13.

Vaidyanathan, *Indian Agriculture Development in a Regional Perspective*, Orient Longman, Hyderabad.

16

Economic Liberalization Policy and Its Impact on Dalits

J.S. SHARMA

Crisis-Driven Reforms

The economic reforms launched in July 1991 in India were in nature of crisis management response to the economic and political crises that erupted in early 1991. The economic crisis comprised a steep fall in the foreign exchange reserve, galloping inflation, large public and current account deficits and mounting Bretton Woods of domestic and foreign debt. In politics, the fall of two governments in a short span of four months, from November 1990 to March 1991; deferment of presentation of the union budget, fairly long political interregnum till the elections, the assassination of a former Prime Minister Rajiv Gandhi in their midst and the emergence of a minority government with a leader sans charisma, reflected an unprecedented crisis. These events led to a sharp erosion of confidence in India among lenders, downgradation of India's credit rating and consequently cut off of international credit lines from private or commercial sources. Indian reforms thus, were essentially of a 'crisis-driven' variety. They did not represent strategic choice with a vision of long term development of Indian people.

Blueprint for the Reforms

The blueprint for the reforms was provided by the combination of macro-economic stabilization and Structural Adjustment Programme (SAP) of International Monetary Fund (IMF) and World Bank respectively, which had been adopted by many countries before in similar situations. The typical measures under these programmes are:

Stabilization

- Devaluation of the currency for making exchange rate more realistic.
- Withdrawal of restrictions on imports.
- Reduction/elimination of fiscal and balance of payments deficits.
- Removal of all controls on prices, exchange and interest rate,
- Elimination/reduction of all subsidies.
- Introduction of financial structure reforms and free entry of foreign financial institutions.
- Complete autonomy of the central bank to pursue independent monetary policy.

Structural Adjustment

- Decontrol of industries.
- Privatization of government-owned entities.
- Structural changes in the economy aimed at export-led growth.
- Free entry of foreign capital and technology without any let, hindrance or conditions.
- Free entry and exit of foreign firms including financial and services industries.
- Free cross-border movement of capital and other funds.
- Legislative safeguards for protection of intellectual property rights.
- Creation of legal climate for enforcement of legal contracts, private property rights, and free entry and exit of business, industrial and financial firms.

The underlying economic philosophy of these programmes is to rely more on market forces, dismantle controls, reduce the role of state, liberalize prices and replace the public with private sector. It is based on the presumption that the public sector leads to inefficient allocation and utilization of economic resources.

Dalits in India

Dalits, as the ex-untouchables prefer to be called, are a very distinct social group. While belonging to a broad class of have-nots, they suffer an additional disability of social oppression. Economically, most of them are still the poorest of poor. The balance minuscule minority has managed to escape poverty limits and to locate itself on to a continuum ranging upto a reasonable level of prosperity. The main factor that has catalysed this transition is the reservation policy, which has provided them a basic opportunity to enter the modern sectors of economy. In social terms however, all Dalits, irrespective of their economic standing, still suffer oppression. This social oppression varies from the crudest variety of untouchability, still being practised in rural areas, to the sophisticated forms of discrimination encountered even in modern sectors of urban areas. Although the statistics indicate that Dalits have made a significant progress on almost all parameters during the five post-independence decades, the relative distance between them and non-Dalit seems to have remained the same or increased. More than 75 per cent of the Dalit workers are still connected with land; 25 per cent being the marginal and small farmers and balance over 50 per cent are the landless labourers. In urban areas, they work mainly in unorganized sector. Out of the total Dalit population of 138 million, the number of Dalits in services falling in the domain of reservations does not exceed 1.1 million; a mere 0.8 per cent.

Corresponding to dual disabilities of Dalits, the main body of the paper is divided in two parts: (i) the impact on Dalits as a part of the class of have-nots, and (ii) the impact on Dalits as a disadvantaged social group. In the first part, impact of the reforms in relation to the two most critical factors affecting the poor people is studied. They are: (i) food security, and (ii) employment poverty, which represents the combined influence of all deprivations, is also reviewed separately. The second part focuses on the influence of the reforms on the specific three disabilities suffered by the Dalits in addition to their poverty. They are: (i) educational backwardness,

(ii) discrimination in employment, and (iii) atrocities and socio-cultural suppression. The last concluding part sums up the study with the observations regarding certain prerequisites for the reforms to be more responsive to the problem of people, particularly Dalits.

Impact of the Reforms on Poor

Food security mainly relates with the production, distribution and pricing of food grains and thus brings agriculture, Public Distribution System (PDS) and the subsidy structure into focus. The reform measures that predominantly affect them are: reduction of fiscal deficit, reduction of subsidies, devaluation of rupee, export orientation and reduction of agricultural credit.

Considering the pattern of the budgetary outlays of the government, the fiscal contraction inevitably resulted in a disproportionate cut in capital expenditure. The capital expenditure slid from 5.10 per cent of GDP in 1990–91 down to 2.74 per cent in 1995–96. In terms of percentage of total expenditure, it fell from an average of 32.8 per cent during the preceding five years of the reforms, to average of 22.05 per cent during the succeeding five years of the reforms. In 1995–96, it was as low as 17.82 per cent.[1] Agriculture sector also bore the share of this cut. The average annual increase in public sector outlay on agriculture and irrigation during 1985–90 fell from Rs 1.3 billion to an average of Rs 0.68 billion during 1990–92. This cut is bound to have a depressing effect on the agricultural production in coming years.

This inherent threat to food security is further magnified by the devaluation of rupee by about 25 per cent effected in July 1991. It resulted in making our food grains cheaper in the international market. As a result, even the ordinary rice (non-aromatic) besides the usually exported super fine aromatic rice (basmati) was exported in huge volumes. The policy impetus to export of rice and wheat is reflected in the actual exports overshooting the targets. For example, in 1995–96 (October-September) actual rice export had reached 5.51 million tonnes as against the target of 2.5 million tonnes. Increasing exports and free market sales of food grains have contributed to a drastic reduction in the stocks of food grains with the public procurement agencies. For example, by September 1996, there was a whooping reduction of 10 million tonnes in the stock of food grains.

In case of wheat, it dipped down to 10.36 million tonnes, even lower than the prescribed minimum norm of 13.1 million tonnes. The policy thrust on agricultural exports has moreover resulted in diversion of land to the export production of non-food primary products. There has been a spurt in corporate farming for export horticulture, floriculture, etc. As per one FAO report, this trend of shifting land for exportable non-food grain crops had already set in, even in the decade ending 1991. The prospects for this trend lies in the fact that there is a huge demand in the developed countries for some 9,000 varieties of edible non-food grain primary products which grow in sub-tropical and tropical regions of the developing countries. Likewise, there is an exportable surplus of food grains and dairy products in the developed countries that craves for markets. Surely, as some economists apprehend, India may turn to be a net importer of food grains is not so a distant future.[2]

The international market for agri-products being a oligopoly of three to six giant companies whose control over the market extends to 80 to 90 per cent,[3] export thrust in this area may not moreover be cost effective. As the experience of some African countries shows, the increasing export of foodgrains for same level of foreign exchange earning certainly impairs the food security of people.

The reforms in banking led to a severe squeeze on agriculture lending. The share of agriculture in net bank credit consistently declined and fell from 17.4 per cent to 12.4 per cent between March 1990 to March 1995. Expressed in constant (1980–81) rupees, it fell from Rs 81,470 million in 1989–90 to Rs 70,500 million in 1994–95. Considering the hike in input costs, the impact of this squeeze could have only been deleterious on food grains production.

As a measure of ensuring food security to the large mass of Indian population, public distribution system was instituted in India in the wake of the calamity of the Great Bengal famine of 1942–43 and the World War II. The system comprises over 4,24,000 fair price shops spread all over the country in rough proportion of the population. The food distributed through PDS is subsidized by the government to the extent of the difference between the issue price of food grains and their economic cost to Food Corporation of India (FCI), the agency which incurs the cost of transportation, storage and administration of the stock of food grain. It devours a significant part of the government subsidy. For example, in 1990–91 out of total food subsidy of Rs 26,000 million, FCI costs amounted to Rs 10,000 million which works out to a whooping 38.5 per cent. With the FCI costs ever-increasing, the impact of any reduction in subsidy has to hit the poor directly.

For ensuring supply of food grains to the PDS system in face of export attraction due to the devaluation of rupee, for maintaining their level of production in spite of sharp rise in input prices and for political consideration of assuaging the rich farmers' lobby, the government had to increase the procurement prices of rice and wheat, 67.56 per cent and 62.8 per cent respectively between 1989–90 and 1993–94. This rise was passed on to the consumers by increasing the issue prices of these commodities by 85.81 per cent and 75.14 per cent respectively between June, 1990 and February, 1994, apparently for reducing the food subsidy. The impact of this rise was reflected in a significant fall in the off-take of food grains. After the reforms, off-take of wheat and rice as a percentage of the allocation has shown considerable decline. In the years from 1990–91 to 1992–93, this percentage was generally over 80 but in the next three years from 1993–94 to 1995–96, it came down to below 50 per cent in case of wheat and to little over 60 per cent in case of rice. The export-attraction of wheat has already led to shortages from situation of surplus, which had to be met with expensive imports. The promising income from wheat crop has resulted in many parts of the country wheat extensively substituting coarse cereals—the main food of poor people, as can be seen from the dwindling output of the latter. The available figures show that it fell from 36.6 million tonnes out of a total food grains output of 179.5 million tonnes in 1992–93 to 30 million tonnes out of a total output of 185 million tonnes in 1995–96.

Since the difference between the consumer-end PDS retail prices and market prices became marginal, the not-so-poor left the PDS and owing to unaffordable prices the poor cut their consumption. The resultant effect on nutrition and hunger had to be borne by the people indirectly proportional to their poverty. One study revealed that the families of landless labourers and marginal and small farmers reduced their off-take by over 50 per cent.[4] Considering their extremely low level of food consumption, below or around the subsistence minimum calories defined by the poverty line, the impact of further reduction of intake by over 50 per cent may have led many people to starvation deaths.

The cumulative effect of the above could be clearly seen in a trend of falling per capita net availability of cereals per day for the Indian population. During two years of the reforms, there was 8.43 per cent fall in per capita availability of cereals and 12.02 per cent fall in that of pulses. Considering the acute inequality of Indian population, the impact of this declining trend on the poorer and disadvantaged sections would be far more severe than indicated by averages. Pulses being the only source of vegetable protein for poor people, a sharp decline in their availability certainly indicates malnutrition.

Employment

The rate of growth of employment in the organized sector dropped from more than 1.7 per cent per annum in the late 1980s to 1.2 per cent in 1991–92 and to 0.6 per cent in 1992–93. Creation of jobs in the public sector fell from 11 million in the preceding four years to 6.2 million in the succeeding four years of the reforms. For the private sector, the corresponding figures rose from 2.08 million to 2.49 million. In the central government establishments, there were 4.03 million jobs on 1st March 1991 which went up next year to 4.14 million. But for the next two years, they came down to 3.97 million and 3.84 million respectively.

Similar picture of declining employment opportunities is held out in the statistics of employment exchanges. The notified vacancies had come down from 0.59 million in 1989–90 to 0.4 million in 1992–93 and to 0.38 million in the subsequent year. Similar decline is seen in the statistics of appointments. The appointments issued during the above three years were 0.29 million, 0.23 million and 0.22 million respectively. The ratios of appointments to the notified vacancies for these years also shows a striking decline, viz., 8.5 per cent, 7.9 per cent and 6.7 per cent respectively.

The contraction in public expenditure and the consequent reduction in aggregate demand could not but adversely affect employment in the unorganized sector, whether non-agricultural rural employment or urban informal sector employment, given the casual nature of such employment.[5]

The policy reforms made benefits of the small sector available to the big industrial houses. National Council of Applied Economic Research had cautioned that the reforms relating to deregulation of the big industries, withdrawal of the license system and global reduction of custom duties would exert adverse impact on the small industries.[6] The statistics of the industrial sickness show a deterioration during the reform period. For example, in 1990, there were 2,21,097 sick industries, which represented a 8.86 per cent decline from the previous year. But after the reforms were launched, this figure went upto 2,23,809 in 1991 and further to 2,47,724 in 1992 indicating the 1.23 per cent and 10.69 per cent growth respectively, over previous years. Entrepreneurship Development Institute of India, Ahmedabad had surveyed the impact of the reforms on small-scale industries in 1993, and observed deterioration in their situation.[7] It attributed this deterioration to three factors (1) general recession in 1991–92, (2) reduction in the budgetary support to the public sector and (3) liberalization of imports of the capital goods. The cumulative impact of these factors has been in the collapse of demand for their products. Small-scale industries based on imports had a tough time due to devaluation of rupee. Increasing competition, increasing costs and pressure on prices has made the very survival difficult for many. In 1994–95 more than 4,00,000 small-scale industries were declared as sick or closed. The reforms in financial sector permitted the banks to charge interest as per the credit rating of debtors and manage their profitability. This also added to the difficulty of small-scale industries, in as much as it became an arduous task to get loans from banks at affordable interest rates. One study clearly concluded that the reforms had an adverse impact on reducing the new job opportunities in the small-scale industries.[8] In rural areas there has been a significant cut in the bank credit to the agriculture and non-agriculture industries. A study on the unemployment in 1993 estimated that out of 25 million unemployed, approximately 10 million came from the unorganized sector of urban areas and the non-agricultural sectors of the rural areas and were the victims of economic reforms.[9]

The economic reforms lay excessive reliance on foreign investment not only for industrial development but also to solve the unemployment problem faced by the country. In this context the observation of United Nations, in the year 1993 Human Development

Report is quite revealing. It says that the Transnational Agro Food Corporations (TNCs) and their associate companies had made significant investments in developing countries but it could not generate significant employment. The amount of jobs created by the foreign investment in the entire Third World during 1990 to 1993 is not even equal to the number of people entering the job market in India in a single year! The companies in the *Fortune 500* list of 1992 together said to have had 5,472 billion dollar sales and 25 million jobs in 1992. Although this sales figure is 27 times India's GDP, the employment figure does not reach even its one-third.

The impetus to export agriculture in the reforms is bringing incorporate and contract system in the agriculture. The government has already declared that the Land Ceiling Act identified as the main obstacle in the process, would be suitably changed. Directionally, the emergent corporate farms will gobble up small holdings of the marginal to middle farmers and push them into the herd of job seeking millions. Corporatization of agriculture always leads to depeasantisation and reduction of labour absorption. The cropping pattern of these capitalist farms makes unskilled agricultural workers redundant. This emergent scenario is certainly going to aggravate the unemployment problem further rather than solving it.

The theme of export-led growth emphasized by the reforms will expose the Indian industry to the vagaries of international markets which can have very negative effect on employment in the long run. Export thrust unmindful of the demands of the domestic requirements can be quite harmful as has been experienced in the case of cotton thread case. In this case, large-scale export of the coarse cotton thread had catapulted 110 weavers in Andhra Pradesh to starvation deaths.[10] There are many such case studies in the international repertoire of experience with such reforms.

The import of modern technology constitutes an important aspect of the economic reforms. Many facilitating provisions have been adopted for attracting the foreign technology and investment. There is a virtual boom in strategic alliances, joint ventures, technological collaborations and inevitable mergers and acquisitions. The influx of foreign brands is bound to displace Indian brands, not by virtue of their intrinsic superiority but because of their sheer financial and organizational muscle. The process will virtually spelled industrialization of the domestic industry. The modern factories replacing them cannot generate even a fraction of the displaced man power. The imperatives of global competitiveness moreover, will increasingly reengineer the business process and curtail employment. The relative mobility of capital vis-à-vis labour also holds an ominous prospect for future jobs.

The buzzword of competition has suddenly awakened one and all but the response everywhere reflects an easy option of cutting the jobs. State owned units are under pressure to reorganize. Nationalized banks have already threatened to declare 4 lakh persons surplus, Railways have stopped recruitment, Department of Post and Tele-communication intend to retrench 2,00,000 workers.[11] The examples indeed are legion. A study conducted by EPW Research Foundation in early 1994 found that the total employment which showed an increase in first two years of the reforms, had slumped thereafter; that the bulk of employment had occurred in contract and other forms of non-regular employment, the share of which in total employment had gradually risen to one-third by March 1993 and that regular employment fell by 3.3 per cent in 1992–93 even as the value of fixed assets of the sample companies rose by some 27 per cent.

Poverty

Poverty is a sum total of all the deprivations. In India, governmental definition of poverty is based on the sole criterion of minimum food requirement for survival. Thus, the poverty line is decided by the income sufficient to buy food equivalent of 2,400 calories in rural and 2,100 calories in urban areas. The data base for poverty estimates is provided by the quinquenial surveys of NSS. NSS also collects the consumer expenditure data by decide group on an annual basis.

The reforms have reversed the two decades long declining trend of poverty. The rural poverty went up from the pre-reform low of 33.7 per cent to 41.7 per cent in 1992 and slightly declined to 40.2 per cent in 1993–94. The urban poverty also showed the same trends hooting up from the pre-reform low of 36 per cent to 37.8 per cent and then coming down to 36.2 per cent. The ratio of ultra poverty to total poverty showed a marked increase after the reforms. In 1990–91, this ratio was 68.95 per cent; it went up to 71.04 per cent in 1991 and to 74.64 per cent in 1992. The corresponding figures for urban areas were 72.99, 73.14 and 74.20 per cent.[12]

In 1992, the rural workers in secondary and tertiary sectors showed a decline of 6.3 per cent and 1.3 per cent respectively from the pre-reform level in 1989–90. Curiously, the primary sector showed a hefty increase of 10.1 per cent in the same period. In rural area about 50 per cent farming households have less than one acre land. They need supplementary work in non-agricultural sector for meeting the two ends. In absence of this work however, they land up engaging themselves with the sundry work related to their tiny farms and declare themselves as the agriculture workers. This increase in the primary sector jobs thus indicates partial unemployment of workforce. The decline in non-agricultural jobs and the overall employment are attributed to the cut in the government expenditure on various poverty alleviation programmes, during the reform period. Notwithstanding their extremely low transfer efficiency[13] and ineffectiveness in targeting the poor, these programmes played a role in poverty reduction during the eighties.

The centre and the state operate them on the 80:20 basis. In the first flush of enthusiasm, the government effected drastic reductions in all of these programmes till it was alarmed by the havoc it created and its political implication in the ensuing general election. It attempted to reverse this trend in 1994–95 and 1995–96 budgets under the much-propagandized 'human face to reforms'. Even after taking all these increased outlays, its resultant effect could be estimated as provision of less than 20 days work at Rs 21 for a person, in a year.

The central transfers constitute a major resource for the states to conduct the programmes under the social sector. These transfers show consistent decline during the reform period on all the heads except for the payment of interest over a period of 1990–91 to 1993–94. This decline amounts to whooping 18.52 per cent. The central assistance to states for some specific schemes likewise has been on consistent decline from much before the start of the reforms but the states seem to have managed the expenditure profile. However, the reform-ethos has eroded this expenditure after 1990–91. The maximum cut was effected in the expenditure on disease-prevention and control programme, which relate with the poverty prone disease like TB, malaria, fileria, leprosy, etc. Its direct manifestation has been aplenty, in form of re-emergence of the epidemics of plague, TB, malaria, jaundice, influenza, pneumonia and very recently, dengue.

Inequality is a corollary of growing poverty. Based on the available data on consumption expenditure, the share of the bottom 30 per cent people, which was growing consistently from 1987–88 upto 1990–91, both in rural as well as in urban areas, had a sudden reversal soon after the reforms were launched. In rural area, it was 15.57 per cent in 1987–88 which rose up to 15.96 per cent in 1990–91, but thereafter slid down to 15.79 per cent in 1991 (July-December) and further to 15.60 per cent in 1992 (July-December). For the urban area, the corresponding figures are 13.33 per cent, 13.74 per cent, 12.74 per cent and 13.17 per cent, indicating a slight upturn in the terminal year. The share of the middle 40 per cent population also dwindled in the same manner in both rural and urban area. The loss of these 70 per cent population appears to have benefited the top 30 per cent population. Their share for the pre-reform period was on consistent decline, had suddenly jumped up in the reform period.

Impact of the Reforms on Dalits as a Disadvantage Social Group

The social disadvantage suffered by Dalits in India was taken note of in the Constitution of India, which was drafted under the chairmanship of Ambedkar—a visionary who had spearheaded the most momentous anti-caste movement of the depressed classes. It provided Dalits with many safeguards, viz., (1) social, educational, cultural and religious safeguards, (2) economic safeguards, (3) political safeguards, and (4) safeguards for employment. The free market ethos of the reforms, conceptually can neither confirm to the democratic spirit of the Indian Constitution of ‘one vote, one value’, nor can it coexist with the system of positive discrimination embodied in these safeguards. For the market grants moneyed person more value, and overtly believes in the jungle law of ‘might is right’. To a large extent, the primary motivation behind these constitutional provisions was liberal democratic aspirations that characterized the freedom movement. However, these aspirations and the initial ideological zeal of the founding fathers withered away in no time and what survived was its utilitarian dimension for the electoral politics. The sorry state of the executive compliance with these constitutional provisions amply bears out the fangs of the Indian society. The reforms will bring a kind of legitimacy to this attitudinal resistance. These safeguards will stand eroded as the reforms gain in momentum. Influence of the reforms is bound to be all pervasive. However, only a few issues of importance to the Dalit masses have been picked up for discussion here.

Reservation and Financial Assistance in Educational Institutions

Reservation in the educational institutions and the financial assistance in the form of scholarships and freeships constitutes perhaps the most important factor in the development scheme for Dalits. For, it is primarily responsible to make the basic input of education available to them. Without education, all the constitutional safeguards including the reservation in services would be infractious. Under this scheme the Dalit students whose parental income is below a specified level, get freeship, reservation in admissions to all the colleges getting grants-in-aid from the government and scholarships. Without this assistance, even today, it would be difficult for Dalits to send their children to school. The reforms have already resulted in freezing the grants to many institutions and in stagnating, if not lowering the expenditure on education. The free market ethos has entered the educational sphere in a big way. Commercialization of education is no more a mere rhetoric, it is now the established fact. Commercial institutions offering specialized education signifying the essential input from utilitarian viewpoint have come up in a big way from cities to small towns. Their product-prices are not only based on the demand-supply consideration in their market segment but also are manipulated by their promotional strategies. In a true spirit of globalization, many foreign universities are invading the educational spheres through hitherto unfamiliar strategic alliances with non-descript commercial agencies, of course at a hefty dollar equivalent prices. Many elite institutions like IIMs, IITs, suddenly facing fund crunch had to raise their fee structure and other prices manifold. They were already beyond the reach of Dalits. When they eventually turn self-financing, their prices would be benchmarked against their international counterparts, which anyway would be affordable to the same top market segment that constitutes the focus of all the reform-talk. As the job markets become acutely competitive, owing to a sharp decline in job opportunities, the polarization between the elite and commoner would also sharpen. Various kinds of price barriers would be erected to thwart the entry of downtrodden.

Even the sphere of primary education the coverage of which has been so miserably in adequate as to leave out multitude of children in villages as illiterate, could not remain unaffected, notwithstanding its already existing divide between the vernacular and English schools. Corporatization has entered this arena, transforming the education into an enterprise for profits. The quality of input these expensive schools will provide will benchmark the products in the contracting job markets. Even today, because of preponderance of the English language in business circles, the divide between village and towns is almost complete in the field of education. It is so difficult for a village student, educated in vernacular medium to compete with his convent educated (now an understatement!) counterpart in cities and towns. If this is the situation of general village population, the plight of Dalits who besides being the poorest of the village population carry additional Bretton Wood of social discrimination, is indeed a worrisome matter. Despite several kinds of state assistance, Dalits are plagued with alarming rate of school dropouts. This may be explained out as much by the need for Dalit children to supplement their meagre family incomes for meeting the two ends as also the erosion of their faith that education could be the instrument to change the pathetic course of their lives. This sense of alienation is going to grow with the progress of the reforms.

Reservations in Services

Whatever may be the other costs, the government policy of reservations in employment sphere has undoubtedly played an important role for Dalits. The policy broadly envisages representation of Dalits in proportion to their population in all the public services which includes the government public sector, autonomous bodies and institutions receiving grant-in-aid from the government. A cursory glance at the figures of this representation is enough to get apathetic state of implementation.

Howsoever, unsatisfactory the results of the implementation may be, the importance of reservations from the Dalit viewpoint cannot be overemphasized. As could be evidenced by the organized private sector, where it would be difficult to find a Dalit employee (save of course in scavenging and menial jobs), without reservations Dalits would have been totally doomed. The importance of reservations thus could only be assessed in relation to situations where they do not exist. Whatever be their defects and deficiencies, they have given certain economic means of livelihood and some social prestige to the sons and daughters of over 1.5 million landless labourers. Whether they get real power or not over 50,000 Dalits could enter the sphere of bureaucratic authority with the help of reservations. Besides these tangible benefits promised by the policy, it has instilled a hope in Dalit community. This hope predominantly manifests in the form of spread of education among them. Their emotional bond with the nation and its Constitution despite heaps of injustice and ignominy they bear every moment of their life may also be significantly attributable to the reservation policy.

The winds of privatization under the economic reforms have already shaken the very foundations of the reservations. The reforms clearly envisage the minimalist government. Wherever the reforms patterned on the structural adjustment programme of the World Bank were carried out, denationalization of the public sector and privatization have come in a big way. Being the late starter, India has not reached the scales achieved by others, say, the Latin American countries. However, the start has not been any unimpressive. Almost all sectors of economy stand opened up for private investment. The disinvestments in existing public sector companies has already been allowed upto 49 per cent by the policy. The publics take being more than 50 per cent the public sector as such is not yet dismantled in policy. It continues to be the state, as before, and hence attracts application of the reservation policy. However, the reform package has already endangered, if not abolished, the reservations through back doors.

In the name of preparing the PSUs for global free market regime, the PSUs are being allowed/encouraged to have strategic alliances with private companies from India and abroad. As such, over the last five years, many profit making PSUs have formed the joint venture companies (JVC). These JVCs are strategically structured as not to fall in the ambit of the PSU-framework. The typical equity stake for the PSU and private could be 49:51. There appears to be a great deal of receptivity for this scheme in the government circles. There are no policy barriers on the business to be pursued by these JVCs. Theoretically, an existing PSU can hive off its business divisions into private JVCs and transform itself into a financial holding company with a skeleton staff. Even if technically it remains a PSU, and assuming that it followed the reservation policy sincerely, it would have little scope to absorb Dalits in its staff. Whatever may be the strategic considerations, the fall out of this process practically amounted to shutting the doors of these new age companies to Dalits and to potential neutralization of the reservation policy.

The policy of limited disinvestments of PSUs not being in conformity with the spirit of the reforms, is bound to be relaxed in favour of privatization any time. But still, all the PSUs may not get privatized at once. The bigger sharks would gobble the better ones up. The worst ones may be closed down or distress-sold. And the middle ones may for quite some time, continue to be the relic of their past. Whatever the scenario, the residual structures of the 'reformed' PSUs are never going to be the same, as far as Dalits are concerned. The ethos of privatization and the excuse of competition, superimposed on the traditional caste prejudice, will never allow reservations to happen, any more.

Other public services are also bound to slip out of the reservation policy. Most of the sectors, which were the traditional domain of the government investment, have already been released for the private investment

Atrocities and Socio-cultural Suppression

The caste atrocities are an integral feature of Dalit life. The government machinery keeps on collecting their statistics year after year and issues it in a report of its Commissioner for SCs and STs (now the National Commission for SCs and STs). There are at least three Articles (15, 17 and 23) in the Constitution of India which seek to mitigate the evil. To give effect to these constitutional provisions the following acts also have been in operation:

1. The Untouchability (Offences) Act, 1955, later amended and re-titled as the Protection of Civil Rights Act, 1955.
2. The Scheduled Castes and Scheduled Tribes (Prevention of Atrocities Act) 1989 and The Bonded Labour System (Abolition) Act, 1976.

Despite this, the statistics of the registered atrocities read like a balance sheet of a blue chip company with consistent rise every successive year. It is pertinent to remember that owing to the dependency relationship of Dalits with the perpetrators of atrocities, not every occurrence of the atrocity gets registered. Rather, it can be safely assumed that behind each registered atrocity over ten atrocity cases go unreported. As per the latest statistics, every day nearly 50 cases of atrocities are registered all over the country. Over three Dalit women are raped and six are disabled on each day round the year. The National Commission analyzed the causes of each of the atrocities in a sample of 45 cases. The analysis shows that out of 45 cases 13 are clearly attributable to the economic reasons. The balance can also be explained out by some kind of weakness of Dalits. Coupled with the weakness of Dalits, their growing assertiveness and refusal to submit to the casteist dictates of the village lords, rebellion ethos assimilated through the Ambedkarian struggle and process of general awareness, also cause atrocities to increase.

The atrocities occur where the dependency relationships are more pronounced and bear economic implications. Villages, where Dalits as landless labourers depend upon landlords or rich farmers for their livelihood and where the traditional caste equations have a potential to yield economic surplus to the latter, provide ideal setting for atrocities. What impact would the new regime have on the socio-economic setting of Indian villages? In face of it, the unbridled capitalism inherent in the reforms is not compatible with any feudal structure. But this thumb rule does not seem to be entirely validated by the developmental experience in India. The capitalism in India did not have to sprout through the bedrock of contradictions of feudalism as in Europe. It was planted in the fertile soil of Indian feudalism. It has grown here on its nutrients. Thus, it would be too mechanical to have a theoretic expectation about the demise of feudalism and hence, the end of the caste through the growth of capitalism. The caste institution moreover, has defied the classical mould of feudalism by possessing many unique features. The most important being its resilience and adaptability. What we experience in the mysterious growth of casteist politics today in India is precisely this ability of caste to adapt to changing times. The annihilation of caste is only possible through economic empowerment of Dalit masses and waging an uncompromising and concerted struggle against its non-economic manifestations.

Can the new regime afford these economic empowerment of Dalits? Can it, for instance, grant them land? Does it have the where withal or motivation to catalyze their struggles against the caste system? The answer to all these questions will be in negative. Instead of talking of land reforms, the new regime will promote depeasantization of Indian agriculture and consolidation of their holdings to start corporate farming. Barring perhaps the example of East Asian countries, the Bretton Wood institutions sponsored reforms have always aggravated the economic inequality everywhere. The experience of other countries where similar reforms were brought in, bears testimony to the fact that with increasing inequality the social tensions also increased as a result of the reforms.

The capital influx in the rural areas will have naturally in the rich farmers who have hegemonic hold over their areas. These sections, will be the main beneficiaries of the improved terms of trade and capitalist development in the rural areas. All the Dalits would be thrown into the job market along with many non-Dalit marginal to middle farmers. The vast army of unemployed thus created by this developmental dynamics will need appropriate instruments for being controlled. The history bear sample testimony to the fact that whenever the people tended to come together with a common identity, the ruling classes have deftly used the time-tested weapon of castes to divide them. Unlike elsewhere, the reforms thus are likely to enliven and rejuvenate the archaic value system.

Conclusion

The economic reforms in the mould of macro-economic stabilization and structural adjustment programme of IMF and World Bank have essentially a pro-rich bias. Wherever they were implemented, they have worsened the situation of the masses of poor people in absolute as well as relative terms. The Dalits in India, being the poorest of the poor have been hit the hardest. Their social disabilities, largely reinforced by and sustained on the economic deprivations, are bound to get accentuated with these policies. The Indian reforms were essentially 'crisis driven' and not 'strategy driven' when they were adopted. There have since been changes in the formation and key persona. The new government for instance has imparted them a form of 'strategy' through their Common Minimum Programme. However, there has not yet been any evidence of this strategy being any different from the course followed by the previous government. The complete discourse of reforms appears to be either grossly off the mark of Indian reality or to assume out its momentous features.

The broad Indian reality is that India has too many poor. As per the Human Development Report, 1996, there are 229 million income poor but more than twice as many, 554 million are capability poor. In terms of capability poverty, its 61.5 per cent population is poor. Its rank according to descending poverty among the 174 countries of the world, is 135. Even 1994–95 India is predominantly an agrarian economy, with over 70 per cent of its population living in villages. No statistics moreover can adequately capture the heinous socio-cultural inequality that is an abiding part of Indian reality. It has acute inequalities not only in economic terms but in the socio-cultural terms.

The free market oriented reform sought to take this grave Indian reality into consideration. Unless there is a wide spread purchasing power in the economy the market can never be free and sustainable. The reform strategy thus should embody sustainable economic empowerment of rural masses; investments to enhance their capability and effective measures for accelerate development of the disadvantaged sections like Dalits. The prerequisite to reforms therefore could be the radical land reforms, massive investments in rural areas into agriculture-related infrastructural projects, universalization of primary education, primary health care system and reinforcement of positive discrimination in favour of Dalits. The devil of casteism could be tamed only by freeing general masses of people from the anxieties and uncertainties about basic survival. The general condition of deprivation has rendered them vulnerable to be the preys to the frequent machinations of the vested interests that make them see the enemy within their own class. The relative equality thus can be the bedrock for launching the socio-cultural offensive, in the form of mass-education programmes. But this all may still not be enough. The policy of positive discrimination in favour of Dalits will have to be reinforced much more vigorously in all the sectors of economy, than ever before. They need to be reframed and simplified for effective implementation. Unlike the current provisions, this may be stopped once their representation comes on par with the general population. The specific reform package can be formulated in terms of the conditions existing then.

Notes

1. Centre for Monitoring the Indian Economy (1996), *Public Finance in India*, June 1996, p. 32.
2. D. Bandyopadhyay, (1995), "Impact of SAP: Hunger and Jobless Growth", *Mainstream*, May 13, 1995, p. 12.
3. United Nations Conference on Trade and Development (1995), *UNCTAD Statistical Pocket Book*, p. 69.
4. Amitava Mukherjee, (1994), Quoted in Bandyopadhyay, D., op. ct., (3), p. 13.
5. Amit Bhaduri and Deepak Nayyar, (1996), *The Intelligent Person's Guide to Liberalization*, Penguin Books, New Delhi, p. 100.
6. National Council of Applied Economic Research (NCAER) and Friedrich-Naumann-Stiftung (1993), *Structure and Promotion of Small Scale Industries in India-Lessons for Future Development*, New Delhi, December 1993.
7. Entrepreneurship Development Institute of India, (1993), Research Report on Impact of New Economic Policies on Small and Tiny Industrial Sector, Ahmedabad, November 1993.
8. M. Bhattacharya, (1994), "Impact of Liberalization on Small Scale Sector", Office of the Development Commissioner, India, New Delhi, *EPW*, p. 1312.
9. Sudipto Mundie, (1993), "Unemployment and Financing of Relief Employment in a Period of Stabilization: India, 1992–94", *Economic and Political Weekly*, January, p. 173.
10. Research Unit of Political Economy (1994), "The Warped Logic of Globalization", *Aspects of India's Economy*, No. 14, July-September 1994, pp. 14–18.
11. Nandita Shah, (1994), quoted in Bandyopadhyay, D., op.ct., (3), p. 15.
12. S., Mahendra Dev, (1995), "Economic Reforms and the Rural Poor", *Economic and Political Weekly*, August 19, p. 2085.
13. Vijay Joshi and I.M.D. Little, (1996), *India's Economic Reforms: 1991–2001*, Oxford University Press, Bombay, pp. 238–39.

Index